Quick After-Work

ASTA
AND
SAUCES
COOKBOOK

Quick After-Work

PASTA
AND
SAUCES
COOKBOOK

JUDY RIDGWAY

FISHER
er
BOOKS™

Publishers:	Bill Fisher	
	Howard Fisher	
	Helen V. Fisher	
North American Editors:	Helen V. Fisher	
	Sarah Smith	
Cover Design:	FifthStreet*design*	
Book Design:	Josh Young	
Illustrations:	Madeleine David	
Book Production:	Deanie Wood	

Library of Congress Cataloging-in-Publication Data

Ridgway, Judy.
  Quick after-work pasta and sauces cookbook / Judy Ridgway.
    p. cm.
  Includes index.
  ISBN 1-55561-089-7 (pb)
  1. Cookery (Pasta). 2. Sauces.
  3. Quick and easy cookery.
  I. Title.
  TX809.M17R53 1996
  641.8' 22—dc20   96-2431
                              CIP

First published in Great Britain in 1993 by Piatkus Books, London
Copyright © 1993 Judy Ridgway
The moral right of the author has been asserted.

North American Edition
Published by Fisher Books
4239 W. Ina Road, Suite #101
Tucson, AZ 85741
(520) 744-6110

© 1996 Fisher Books
Printed in USA
Printing 10 9 8 7 6 5 4 3 2 1

Contents

INTRODUCTION

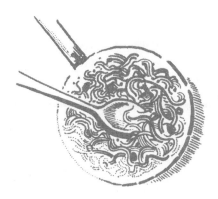

I was a bit of a latecomer to pasta but, like many converts, I am now quite fanatical about it. Pasta is as delicious served with a simple vegetable sauce as with salmon or shellfish. It makes a quick and easy supper dish or it can form part of a grand dinner. Pasta never takes more than 15 minutes to cook and many sauces can be cooked in the same time.

My inspiration for these sauces is mainly Italian, probably because I began to enjoy pasta during visits to Italy. The first time I was presented with a mountain of genuine Italian pasta, I was in a local restaurant in a village near Amalfi in the Bay of Naples and pasta was the only choice. The food was cooked by the owner in a tiny kitchen at the back of the restaurant and the aromas were enticing. After serving us, the waiter stood expectantly. Not wanting to disappoint him, I valiantly dug in. It was delicious and I was hooked!

I was struck, both then and on subsequent visits, by the way Italian cooks use punchy flavors with pasta. I have striven to capture this intensity of flavor in the sauces in this book and hope that I have succeeded. Luckily for today's home cook, slow cooking is not the only way to distill the flavors of a dish; speedy reduction at high temperatures can work just as well.

Since that vacation in the Bay of Naples I have driven down the toe and heel of Italy, looked at olive groves in Abruzzo and studied wine in Tuscany and Piedmont. There have also been visits to the Italian lakes, holidays in Liguria and business meetings in Rome and Milan. On all these trips I made notes on the classic sauces and asked chefs, friends and colleagues for their own favorite recipes.

Other ideas for sauces came from the Middle and Far East, where egg noodles are almost as popular as pasta is in Italy. A recent visit to North America added some interesting variations on the Italian classics. And I have experimented with my own favorite ingredients to come up with the rest of the recipes.

The beauty of pasta dishes is that they are complete and require nothing else. But if you would like to serve a salad too, I have given some suggestions for combinations that work particularly well. Some people like to use bread to mop up any extra sauce.

Pasta is a convenient and enjoyable way of following nutritionists' exhortations to eat more cereals. If you choose whole-wheat pasta you will increase the fiber content of the meal even more. In addition, pasta contains B-complex vitamins and some minerals.

Many people believe that pasta is fattening. However it is not the pasta itself which sends the calories shooting up, but the fat content of the sauce you toss it in. You generally do not need large quantities of oil to dress pasta—a tablespoonful will do. Nor do you need to use too much fat in the sauce. If you are tossing the pasta in a sauce it does not need to be dressed with oil as well. When cooked, a 3-oz. (85g) portion of pasta on its own yields about 120 calories.

It is no longer true that people with a wheat or gluten allergy are unable to eat pasta. Health-food stores now carry pasta made of rice, millet, barley and spelt. Of these I recommend spelt, which can be eaten by people with a wheat allergy and has a low gluten content. Its quite strong flavor overpowers some of the lighter sauces, but it cooks exactly like wheat pasta and you can achieve the same kind of *al dente* texture. The others are easy to overcook. The rice and millet spirals I tried became sticky within 3 minutes so they need very careful timing. However the flavor was not as overpowering.

It is said that in Italy there are enough kinds of pasta to serve a different one every day. Elsewhere the choice may be slightly narrower but there are still a great many from which to choose. The big question these days is whether to buy fresh or dried pasta. Since the former seems to have become fashionable, traditional dried-pasta manufacturers are offering ever more types of fresh pasta.

Many people seem to think that fresh pasta is more authentic than dried. However this is just not true. A certain amount of special local-style pasta is still made in the home but it is only in Northern Italy that fresh pasta is offered for sale. Southern Italy is the home of dried-pasta production and huge quantities are sold there.

Certain types of pasta lend themselves to particular sauces and so I have arranged this book by pasta style rather than by ingredients. Particularly quick pasta sauces are in Chapter 1.

There are no hard-and-fast rules about which sauce you should serve with what pasta and there is no pressing reason why you should not break with tradition and serve a Pesto Sauce with fusilli or a Carbonara Sauce with spaghetti. Very often the choice actually depends on what you have in stock! Nevertheless, I think long round pasta does work particularly well with oil-based sauces and that tubular pasta tastes better with a rich or thick sauce which will partially fill the hollows.

In addition to being quick and easy to cook, dried pasta is also convenient to store. It will keep for a year or more if kept dry, and it is ready to cook straight from the package. At any one time I usually have a couple of long pastas from which to choose, one variety of tubular pasta and some pasta shapes. Of course you don't need to have so many different pastas in your pantry—one will do. But if you are anything like me you will find that the more you get into pasta the more you want to experiment with all the different lengths, shapes and sizes!

ABOUT THE AUTHOR

Judy Ridgway is a British author of more than two dozen books, including the international bestseller *Vegetarian Gourmet*. She was cooking editor for *Woman's World* for six years, and a wine columnist on *Woman and Home* for four years.

As well as writing features on food, wine, cookery and travel for a variety of newspapers and magazines, Judy appears on British television and regularly takes part in national and local radio interviews and phone-ins. She has traveled extensively and shares recipes and tips from many countries.

Judy's other books include: *Quick After-Work Vegetarian Cookbook* (also available in a North American edition from Fisher Books), *Vegetarian Delights, The Vegetable Year, Salad Days, Vegetarian Wok Cookery, The Complete Cheese Cookbook* and *The Pocket Book of Oils, Vinegars and Seasonings*.

NUTRIENT ANALYSIS

Nutrient analysis was calculated using The Food Processor® for Windows software program, version 6.0, copyright 1987-1995 by ESHA Research.

Analysis does not include optional ingredients or variations. Where an ingredient amount is a range, the higher number is used.

The following abbreviations are used:

Cal = Calories   **Tot. Fat** = Total Fat
Prot = Protein   **Sat. Fat** = Saturated Fat
Carb = Carbohydrates   **Chol** = Cholesterol
Fib = Fiber

COOKING PASTA

Pasta is very quick and easy to prepare—even the thickest of dried pastas cooks in 15 minutes. Fresh pasta cooks in 2 or 3 minutes. Overcooking is the only danger. It is a good idea to test the pasta 1-2 minutes before the cooking time is up.

Everyone has heard the phrase *al dente,* meaning "firm to the bite," and this is essential for pasta. Overcooked pasta will be sticky and unpleasant. Be sure to drain immediately after cooking.

QUANTITIES

The first step is to decide upon the quantity to be used. Appetites vary but here are my recommendations for pasta for four people in a variety of different serving situations:

	Dry	Fresh
Pasta as a main dish	12 oz. (340g)	2 lb. (900g)
Pasta as a starter	6-8 oz. (175-225g)	1 to 1-1/4 lb. (450-600g)
Pasta as a side dish	8 oz. (225g)	1-1/4 lb. (600g)

Most of the recipes in this book are designed to serve four people as a main course or six people as a starter. In one or two cases smaller quantities than those given above are specified for a particular recipe; this is because the classic dish uses a lower ratio of pasta to sauce. If you are cooking for a buffet party you can double the quantities but remember that people usually do not eat as much standing up as they do sitting down.

COOKING METHOD

Whether it's fresh or dried, pasta needs plenty of boiling water. Allow at least 2 quarts (2.5 liters) water for 8 oz. (225g) pasta. If you use too little water the pasta will stick to itself and to the bottom of the pan.

1. Fill a large pan with salted water and add a teaspoon of olive oil. Bring the water to a fast boil.

2. Add pasta to the boiling water gradually so the water keeps boiling. Let long pieces of pasta curl around the pan as they soften.

3. Cook pasta uncovered at a steady boil, testing after three-quarters of the cooking time. Overcooked pasta will be very sticky.

4. When the pasta is cooked, drain in a colander and then toss at once with your chosen dressing or sauce. Do not let cooked pasta stand alone or it will start to stick together.

COOKING TIMES

Long thin dried pasta will take 4-5 minutes, spaghetti and tagliatelle 8-12 minutes and shapes as long as 12-15 minutes. Different brands may vary in their cooking times but they usually have cooking instructions. Follow these carefully and you will not go wrong.

Fresh pasta will take 2-3 minutes, although stuffed pasta like tortelloni may take a little longer. These will usually be cooked through when they rise and float on top of the cooking water.

THE FINAL TOUCH

Freshly grated Parmesan cheese is the traditional accompaniment, except with fish. Freshly ground black pepper is usually offered as well. Sprigs of fresh herbs are the modern garnish and, if carefully chosen to complement the sauce, can be very good indeed. Other accompaniments include chili oil, freshly grated Pecorino cheese or a few drops of Tabasco® sauce.

Some of the recipes include toasted nuts or pine nuts (piñon or pignalia) as a garnish or as part of the basic dish. Toasting brings out the flavor; the best way is to dry-fry them in a hot skillet until lightly browned. Keep them moving in the hot pan or they will burn.

POPULAR PASTA SHAPES

LONG ROUND

Bigoli

Capelli D'Angelo

Spaghetti

Spaghettini

Tonnarelli

Vermicelli

LONG FLAT

Fettuccine

Curly Lasagne

Linguine

Noodles

Pappardelle

Tagliatelle

Trenette

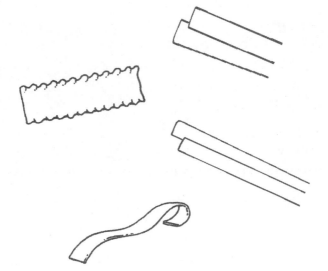

TUBULAR

Bucatini

Garganelli

Macaroni

Penne

Rigatoni

Ziti

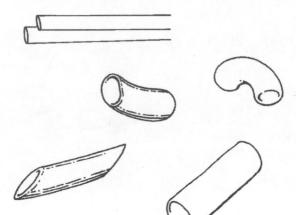

PASTA SHAPES

Cavatieddi

Conchiglie

Farfalle

Fusilli

Orecchiette

Rotelle

Chapter One

EXTRA-QUICK SAUCES

All the recipes in this book are quick; those in this chapter enable you to get a meal onto the table in record time. Bread and a simple side salad are optional accompaniments.

You can serve these sauces with any kind of pasta. If your pantry offers a choice of pasta, try the oil-based and butter-based sauces with spaghetti, the cream-based sauces with long flat pasta and the other types of sauces with shapes or tubular pasta.

Ready-made stuffed pasta such as ravioli and tortelloni are often especially quick to cook and usually need only the addition of a simple oil, butter or cream dressing, perhaps with some fresh herbs.

OIL-BASED SAUCES

Olive oil is the first choice for a quick pasta dressing in Central and Southern Italy. The pasta is tossed in a full and fruity extra-virgin oil and piled up in the serving dishes. Next comes the freshly grated Parmesan cheese and perhaps, but by no means as frequently as Italian restaurants outside Italy would have you believe, some freshly ground black pepper.

Oil makes a good dressing for pasta because it helps keep the pasta from sticking together. It also carries the flavor of other ingredients well. The simplest and quickest of dishes is made by gently heating lightly crushed cloves of garlic in a well-flavored olive oil. The garlic should not burn. Strain the oil and use it to dress the pasta.

Dried and slightly crushed chiles are often added in Southern Italy, where a piquant flavor is greatly appreciated. You could use chili powder or a few drops of Tabasco instead. This dish is usually served without cheese but you might add a handful of chopped fresh parsley. The Italians maintain that this dish is a great hangover cure—if you eat it before you go to bed!

Other very quick ideas include tossing pasta in sun-dried-tomato, artichoke or olive paste with additional olive oil and perhaps a few fried onion slices or some garlic.

Nut oil, sesame oil and unrefined cold-pressed sunflower oil have definite flavors of their own and can be used with great effect to add interest to pasta dishes. Try tossing cooked pasta in almond oil and then serve with a sprinkling of toasted almond flakes. Or use a few drops of roasted sesame oil in a bland corn or sunflower oil and toss with pasta and fresh herbs.

Extra-Virgin Olive Oil ~ *This top grade of olive oil is used as a condiment and flavoring in its own right. Ordinary olive oil is used for cooking when you do not particularly want the flavor of olives.*

Olives for extra-virgin oil are cold-pressed in hydraulic presses and the oil is unrefined. Olives are grown all over Italy, Spain, Greece and Portugal and in Southern France. Each region produces oil with its own distinctive flavor. Some are quite mild and sweet. Others are more pungent, often with a peppery note to them. Choose your oil to match the other ingredients in the dish and use the same oil to dress a side salad. Olives are also grown in California.

ANCHOVY-AND-GARLIC SAUCE

This is a classic Italian sauce from the South, where it is usually served with long round pasta. It has a punchy but not overpowering flavor. If you think the anchovies will be too strong for you, rinse them in cold water before using. For an even milder taste, soak them in milk for a few minutes before draining, drying and chopping.

6 tablespoons olive oil

3 cloves garlic, peeled and crushed

1 can (2-oz. / 60g) anchovy fillets, drained and chopped

Cooked pasta to serve 4 people

Freshly ground black pepper

Variation

Add a spoonful of capers or chopped black olives to the pasta.

1. Heat oil in a saucepan and sauté garlic for 1 minute.

2. Add anchovies and continue cooking 1-2 minutes over medium heat until fish flakes, making a creamy sauce.

3. Toss pasta in this sauce and serve with freshly ground black pepper.

Makes 4 servings.

Each serving contains:

Cal	Prot	Carb	Fib	Tot. Fat	Sat. Fat	Chol	Sodium
329	8g	24g	1g	22g	3g	12mg	521mg

ORIENTAL OYSTER-MUSHROOM SAUCE

Oyster mushrooms cook in a flash, so be careful not to overcook them. Do not serve cheese with this sauce; it simply doesn't work. Instead serve a salad of shredded cilantro leaves, bean sprouts and grated carrot tossed in a vinaigrette flavored with a few drops of sesame oil.

3/4 lb. (340g) oyster mushrooms

1/4 cup (60ml) olive oil

1 clove garlic, peeled and crushed (optional)

1 large bunch fresh chives, chopped

1 tablespoon soy sauce

1/4 cup (60ml) orange juice

1 tablespoon grated orange peel

Pinch of Chinese five-spice powder

Cooked pasta to serve 4 people

Variations

1. Add sliced peel from 3 kumquats with orange peel.
2. Instead of Chinese five-spice powder, add 1 teaspoon roasted sesame oil and sprinkle with toasted sesame seeds.

1. Roughly chop mushrooms just before starting to cook.
2. Heat oil in a large frying pan and gently sauté the garlic, if using, and half the chives for 1 minute.
3. Add soy sauce, orange juice and orange peel and bring to a boil. Continue cooking for 2-3 minutes to reduce a little.
4. Add Chinese five-spice powder and mushrooms and toss all together over medium heat for about 1 minute. Spoon over pasta, sprinkle with remaining chives and serve at once.

Makes 4 servings.

Each serving contains:

Cal	Prot	Carb	Fib	Tot. Fat	Sat. Fat	Chol	Sodium
273	7g	30g	3g	15g	2g	0mg	207mg

LIGURIAN SAUCE

This recipe uses ingredients similar to those in Pesto Sauce, a Ligurian specialty, but is even quicker to make. Serve with a simple tomato salad.

1/4 cup (60ml) olive oil

1/4 cup (60g) pine nuts, toasted (page xiv)

Pinch of salt

2-3 tablespoons chopped fresh basil leaves

1-2 cloves garlic, peeled and minced

Cooked pasta to serve 4 people

Freshly grated Parmesan cheese

1. Heat oil in a large pan and add remaining ingredients except pasta and cheese. Cook for 1 minute.

2. Toss pasta in the mixture and serve with Parmesan cheese.

Makes 4 servings.

Each serving contains:

Cal	Prot	Carb	Fib	Tot. Fat	Sat. Fat	Chol	Sodium
347	10g	27g	2g	24g	4g	5mg	185mg

PIMENTO-AND-SALAMI SAUCE

Pimento paste is available in gourmet shops and Italian grocers. It is made from sweet peppers and is not at all hot. If you cannot find it, substitute minced pimentos. Serve this dish with a salad of lettuce and watercress.

Cooked pasta to serve 4 people

1/4 cup (60ml) olive oil, warmed

1 (2-oz.) jar pimento paste or pimentos, minced

3 oz. (85g) salami, diced

20 large salted capers, soaked in water and drained

1. Toss pasta in the oil and add pimento paste or minced pimentos and salami.
2. Toss again and serve sprinkled with capers.

Makes 4 servings.

Each serving contains:

Cal	Prot	Carb	Fib	Tot. Fat	Sat. Fat	Chol	Sodium
298	7g	25g	2g	19g	4g	14mg	489mg

SYRIAN SAUCE

This Middle Eastern sauce is usually used with a tubular pasta such as macaroni. It is very aromatic and goes well with kebabs.

1/4 cup (60ml) olive oil

1 onion, peeled and minced

2 cloves garlic, peeled and minced

2 tablespoons chopped fresh parsley

1 teaspoon chopped fresh mint

1/4 teaspoon ground cinnamon

Salt and pepper to taste

Cooked pasta to serve 4 people as a starter or side dish

Fresh parsley sprigs

1. Heat oil in a saucepan and sauté onion and garlic until they are golden brown.
2. Stir in all the other ingredients except parsley. Toss well together. Serve garnished with sprigs of fresh parsley.

Makes 4 servings.

Variation

Garnish with raisins and toasted pine nuts (page xiv).

Each serving contains:

Cal	Prot	Carb	Fib	Tot. Fat	Sat. Fat	Chol	Sodium
212	3g	19g	1g	14g	2g	0mg	68mg

BUTTER-BASED SAUCES

Butter is used in Northern Italy but rarely in Central and Southern Italy. In Milan long pasta tossed in melted butter and grated Parmesan cheese is sometimes known as *Inglese* or English sauce. Add a little sage and black pepper for a classic dressing for plain or stuffed pasta. Nutmeg also marries well with butter.

HAM-AND-CHEESE SAUCE

Simple, easily available ingredients make this a good standby on busy evenings. The sauce will probably be ready before the pasta! So while you're waiting, prepare a simple green salad to accompany it.

6 tablespoons (75g) unsalted butter

3 oz. (85g) cooked ham, diced

4 oz. (115g) freshly grated Parmesan cheese (1 cup)

Cooked pasta to serve 4 people

Salt and pepper to taste

1. Melt butter in a saucepan and stir in the ham and cheese. Cook and stir until cheese is melted.
2. Add pasta to the pan, season to taste and toss all together.

Makes 4 servings.

Variation

Omit ham and use toasted pine nuts (page xiv) for texture.

Each serving contains:

Cal	Prot	Carb	Fib	Tot. Fat	Sat. Fat	Chol	Sodium
433	21g	25g	1g	28g	17g	80mg	920mg

HUNGARIAN POPPY-SEED SAUCE

Toasted poppy seeds are popular in Hungary, where they are used in all kinds of savory dishes as well as on cakes and bread. Here they add crunchy texture and unusual flavor.

6 tablespoons (75g) butter

2 tablespoons poppy seeds, toasted (page xiv)

Cooked pasta to serve 4 people

Freshly grated Parmesan cheese

1. Melt butter in a large saucepan. Add poppy seeds and pasta and toss well together.
2. Serve with freshly grated Parmesan cheese.

Makes 4 servings.

Variation

Reduce the quantity of butter and add a little cream.

Each serving contains:

Cal	Prot	Carb	Fib	Tot. Fat	Sat. Fat	Chol	Sodium
324	8g	25g	2g	22g	12g	52mg	294mg

QUICK SHRIMP SAUCE

Nutmeg is the surprise ingredient in this elegant sauce. Serve with a long pasta for a contrast in textures.

1/2 cup (125g) unsalted butter
6 oz. (175g) cooked, peeled shrimp
Freshly ground black pepper
A generous sprinkling of grated nutmeg
Cooked pasta to serve 4 people
Chopped fresh parsley

1. Melt butter in a large saucepan and add shrimp, pepper and nutmeg.

2. Toss with pasta and serve at once, sprinkled with chopped fresh parsley.

Makes 4 servings.

Each serving contains:

Cal	Prot	Carb	Fib	Tot. Fat	Sat. Fat	Chol	Sodium
365	13g	24g	1g	24g	15g	145mg	99mg

CREAM-BASED SAUCES

Cream and pasta make a great combination. All kinds of simple flavorings can be added to cream to make a quick sauce. If you feel that cream alone is too rich for you, combine it with a good stock and boil rapidly to thicken. Then toss in some diced artichoke hearts, fresh peas or shredded spinach and you have a sauce fit for a dinner party.

Yogurt can be used in place of some or all of the cream but it will need to be stabilized with a little cornstarch or potato starch. The flavor will, of course, be quite different. Use strained yogurt for a creamier texture.

PARSLEY-TARRAGON CREAM SAUCE

Almost any combination of fresh herbs can be used. Instead of parsley or tarragon try chervil, dill or thyme. Serve with a mixed-green salad.

1 cup (250ml) whipping cream
2 tablespoons condensed vegetable or chicken stock
Salt and pepper to taste
2 tablespoons chopped fresh parsley
2 tablespoons chopped fresh tarragon
Cooked pasta to serve 4 people

1. Place cream, stock, salt and pepper in a saucepan and bring to a boil.
2. After about 3 minutes add the chopped herbs and continue cooking over a fairly high heat.
3. When sauce thickens, taste and adjust seasoning. Pour over the pasta, toss and serve.

Makes 4 servings.

Each serving contains:

Cal	Prot	Carb	Fib	Tot. Fat	Sat. Fat	Chol	Sodium
328	6g	26g	1g	23g	14g	82mg	138mg

GREEN-PEPPERCORN SAUCE

I usually make this sauce with fresh green peppercorns, which are very aromatic and spicy; if you use bottled peppercorns you may need to add more. Fresh peppercorns blacken quickly so use as soon after purchase as possible.

2 tablespoons (25g) fresh green peppercorns or 1-1/2 oz. (45g) bottled green peppercorns

2 tablespoons (25g) butter

1 clove garlic, peeled and crushed

1 cup (250ml) whipping cream

Cooked pasta to serve 4 people

1. Strip fresh peppercorns from their stalks, or rinse bottled peppercorns.

2. Gently sauté peppercorns in butter for 5-6 minutes, until they begin to pop. Try not to burn the butter.

3. Stir in garlic, cook 1 minute and add cream. Bring to a boil and cook another 2-3 minutes. Toss with the pasta and serve at once.

Makes 4 servings.

Each serving contains:

Cal	Prot	Carb	Fib	Tot. Fat	Sat. Fat	Chol	Sodium
377	5g	26g	1g	28g	17g	97mg	82mg

RED-ONION SAUCE

Red onions add a pretty pink color to this well-flavored sauce from Northern Italy. Serve with long pasta and a colorful mixed-green salad.

1/4 cup (50g) butter

2 cloves garlic, peeled and chopped

1 large red onion, peeled and minced

1 large bunch of Italian parsley, roughly chopped

Pinch of dried marjoram

Salt and pepper to taste

1/2 cup (125ml) whipping cream

Cooked pasta to serve 4 people

Freshly grated Parmesan cheese

1. Melt butter in a deep pan and gently sauté garlic and onion for 3 minutes. Do not allow them to burn.

2. Add herbs, salt, pepper and cream and bring to a boil. Simmer 2-3 minutes.

3. Toss pasta in sauce and serve with grated Parmesan cheese on the side.

Makes 4 servings.

Each serving contains:

Cal	Prot	Carb	Fib	Tot. Fat	Sat. Fat	Chol	Sodium
118	1g	4g	1g	12g	7g	31mg	119mg

CREAMED-PROSCIUTTO SAUCE

This rich sauce is excellent with long flat or tubular pasta. It is much easier to chop the prosciutto if you ask the butcher to cut it in one thick piece rather than in the usual thin slices.

1/4 cup (50g) butter

1/2 cup (125ml) whipping cream

2 oz. (60g) prosciutto or Parma ham, minced

Grated nutmeg

Salt and freshly ground black pepper

3 oz. (85g) freshly grated Parmesan cheese (3/4 cup)

Cooked pasta to serve 4 people

1. Melt butter in a large saucepan and add cream. Bring mixture to a boil and cook for 1 minute.

2. Add prosciutto, nutmeg, salt and pepper. Check the balance of flavors, then add cheese.

3. Toss pasta in the sauce and serve at once with more black pepper and Parmesan cheese on the side.

Makes 4 servings.

Each serving contains:

Cal	Prot	Carb	Fib	Tot. Fat	Sat. Fat	Chol	Sodium
440	16g	26g	1g	30g	18g	95mg	794mg

GOAT-CHEESE-AND-WALNUT SAUCE

This smooth and creamy sauce is accented by walnuts. Serve with a delicate salad of lamb's lettuce or baby spinach dressed with walnut oil.

6 oz. (175g) goat cheese
1/2 cup (125ml) whipping cream
Salt and pepper to taste
Cooked pasta to serve 4 people
1/2 cup (50g) walnuts, chopped

1. Melt cheese in the cream over low heat and bring to a boil. Season to taste.
2. Toss pasta and walnuts in the sauce and serve at once.

Makes 4 servings.

Each serving contains:

Cal	Prot	Carb	Fib	Tot. Fat	Sat. Fat	Chol	Sodium
485	17g	28g	2g	34g	16g	78mg	848mg

CREAMED-FETA-AND-OLIVE SAUCE

Various soft cheeses can be used in this recipe. Try Mozzarella with tubular pasta or Brie with a long thin pasta such as vermicelli or linguine. Serve as a starter with a sliced-tomato-and-onion salad.

1 cup (250ml) whipping cream

1/4 lb. (115g) feta cheese, crumbled (1 cup)

12 black olives, pitted and chopped

Leaves from 4 large sprigs of basil, roughly torn

Freshly ground black pepper

Cooked pasta to serve 4 as a starter

1. Heat cream in a saucepan and bring to a boil. Cook for a few minutes to reduce.

2. Add feta cheese and continue cooking, stirring constantly, until cheese has partially melted.

3. Stir in remaining ingredients. Toss well together and serve with more freshly ground black pepper.

Makes 4 servings.

Each serving contains:

Cal	Prot	Carb	Fib	Tot. Fat	Sat. Fat	Chol	Sodium
376	8g	20g	1g	30g	18g	107mg	457mg

RICOTTA-AND-TOMATO SAUCE

Any kind of ricotta cheese can be used for this recipe. You can also substitute cottage cheese. A side salad of baby spinach leaves or watercress makes the ideal accompaniment.

1/2 cup (125ml) whipping cream

5 oz. (150g) ricotta or cottage cheese, crumbled (2/3 cup)

3 ripe tomatoes, seeded and chopped

Salt and pepper to taste

Cooked pasta to serve 4 people

1. Gently heat cream in a large saucepan. Add cheese and continue cooking for 2 minutes until very hot.

2. Stir in tomatoes, salt and pepper. Add pasta and toss all together. Serve with more freshly ground black pepper.

Makes 4 servings.

Variation

Substitute 3/4 cup (75g) coarsely chopped walnuts for the tomatoes and add mascarpone instead of the cream.

Each serving contains:

Cal	Prot	Carb	Fib	Tot. Fat	Sat. Fat	Chol	Sodium
304	9g	30g	2g	16g	10g	59mg	117mg

SHRIMP-AND-GARLIC SAUCE

You can use any kind of garlic-flavored cheese for this well-flavored quickie. Boursin, Bressot or garlic roulade all work well. Serve with long flat pasta for the best results.

6 oz. (175g) Boursin cheese
  (1-1/2 cups)

3 tablespoons whipping cream

1/4 lb. (115g) cooked, peeled
  shrimp

Freshly ground black pepper

Cooked pasta to serve 4 people

Chopped fresh parsley

1. Heat cheese and cream in a small saucepan. Stir until cheese has melted. Bring to a boil and remove from the heat.
2. Stir in shrimp and pepper. Toss together and pour over the pasta. Serve sprinkled with the chopped parsley.

Makes 4 servings.

Each serving contains:

Cal	Prot	Carb	Fib	Tot. Fat	Sat. Fat	Chol	Sodium
324	11g	26g	1g	20g	12g	96mg	170mg

VESUVIO SAUCE

This opulent recipe is the house specialty of Vesuvio, a popular Italian restaurant on the Croisette in Cannes. You can economize by buying smoked salmon trimmings but whole slices look better. Lightly steamed sugar peas make a good accompaniment.

1 cup (250ml) whipping cream
2 tablespoons (25g) butter
Salt to taste
12-14 whole black peppercorns
1/4 lb. (115g) smoked salmon
Cooked pasta to serve 4 people

1. Put cream, butter and salt into a large saucepan and bring to a boil. Simmer 5 minutes, stirring occasionally.
2. Meanwhile pan-fry peppercorns or toast them under the broiler.
3. Cut smoked salmon into 2-inch (5cm) strips and add to cream mixture. Stir and add pasta.
4. Toss and serve, garnished with toasted peppercorns.

Makes 4 servings.

Each serving contains:

Cal	Prot	Carb	Fib	Tot. Fat	Sat. Fat	Chol	Sodium
409	11g	26g	1g	30g	18g	104mg	371mg

EGG-BASED SAUCES

Beaten egg added to piping-hot pasta will cook in the residual heat. If the pasta has cooled too much, a touch of heat to the base of the pan will do the trick. Work as fast as you can, tossing the mixture so the egg coats all the strands. If you take too long the egg will sink to the bottom of the pan and set there.

EGG-AND-CAPER SAUCE

This recipe comes from a Canadian friend living in Rome. She uses this mixture with fairly thin pasta such as trenette or linguine but you could also use fettuccine.

3 eggs, beaten
1 tablespoon capers, drained
Salt and pepper to taste
1/4 lb. (115g) Pecorino Romano cheese, finely grated (1 cup)
2 tablespoons (25g) butter
Cooked pasta to serve 4 people

1. Mix eggs with capers, salt, pepper and half the cheese and beat well together.
2. Heat butter in a large saucepan and add the pasta. Stir until heated.
3. Pour egg-cheese mixture over hot pasta. Toss together. Serve with black pepper and remaining cheese.

Makes 4 servings.

Each serving contains:

Cal	Prot	Carb	Fib	Tot. Fat	Sat. Fat	Chol	Sodium
336	18g	26g	1g	18g	10g	204mg	593mg

EGG-AND-TARRAGON SAUCE

Egg and tarragon make an excellent combination but you can use parsley, dill or chervil if tarragon is not available. Serve with a radicchio salad dressed with extra-virgin olive oil.

3 eggs, beaten

Salt and pepper to taste

1 tablespoon chopped fresh
  tarragon

2-3 green onions, minced

4 oz. (115g) Parmesan cheese,
  finely grated (1 cup)

2 tablespoons (25g) butter

Cooked long pasta to serve
  4 people

1. Mix eggs with salt, pepper, tarragon, green onions and half the cheese and beat well together.

2. Melt butter in a large saucepan and add the pasta. Stir until heated through.

3. Pour egg-cheese mixture over hot pasta and toss together. Serve with black pepper and remaining cheese.

Makes 4 servings.

Each serving contains:

Cal	Prot	Carb	Fib	Tot. Fat	Sat. Fat	Chol	Sodium
359	21g	27g	1g	19g	10g	197mg	702mg

Parmesan Cheese ~ *Parmesan is the English name given to Parmigiana Reggiano, a cheese from Parma in Emilia Romagna. The cheese is aged for at least a year before it is sold and it hardens and improves in flavor as it matures. Always buy Parmesan in a single piece and grate it just before you need it. Ready-grated cheese lacks flavor.*

Chapter Two

LONG ROUND PASTA

Long round pasta in the form of spaghetti is without doubt the best-known style of pasta outside Italy. It is very versatile and can be served with almost any kind of sauce. All the sauces in Chapter 1 work well with it. However, light oil-based sauces are particularly good because they allow the strands to remain separate and slippery.

All the types of long round pasta listed on the next page are available dried; quite a few of them are also available fresh. Many can be found in whole-wheat versions but these are not Italian in origin. Bigoli is the only pasta traditionally made with whole-wheat flour.

You can also buy brands of spaghetti flavored with tomato, mushrooms and even truffles, but I find them rather bitter and prefer to add these flavors by way of the sauce.

For cooking instructions, see page xiii.

SPAGHETTI—There is some variation in the length of this long and fairly thin round pasta. I remember when stores only sold spaghetti which was at least 16 inches (40cm) long but now there is a trend toward shorter lengths of 10 inches (25cm) or 12 inches (30cm).

SPAGHETTINI—This thinner version of medium-length spaghetti is often used for fish-based or seafood sauces.

VERMICELLI—This name is used for spaghettini in Southern Italy. Some producers make an even finer, threadlike pasta which they call *vermicelli* but which is more like capelli d'angelo.

CAPELLI D'ANGELO—*Angel hair* is the English translation for this extremely thin threadlike pasta. It is usually served with a very light sauce or in soup.

TONNARELLI—A home-made square spaghetti. In Abruzzo it is known as *maccheroni alla chitarra*. It is interchangeable with round spaghetti.

BIGOLI—Originating in the region around Venice, this is the only traditional Italian pasta made with whole-wheat flour. It is long and thick and the dough is bound with eggs—often duck eggs.

TOMATO SAUCE

Wherever you go in Italy you can be sure that the chefs and cooks will offer you their own versions of tomato sauce (*salsa di pomodoro*). Using the ripest tomatoes available, they add fresh herbs, lemon zest and chile peppers for even more flavor. More-substantial sauces use olives, tuna or prosciutto (raw cured ham). Italy's sunshine seems to be distilled into their tomatoes so, if you can, use Italian plum tomatoes.

CLASSIC TOMATO SAUCE

This classic sauce has a more-complex flavor than the simple sauces, but does not take much longer to make. It freezes well for future use. Serve as is or flavored with fresh or dried herbs.

1 small onion, peeled and minced

3 tablespoons olive oil

1 small carrot, peeled and minced

2 stalks celery, trimmed and minced

1 can (20-oz. / 600g) chopped tomatoes

Salt and pepper to taste

Cooked pasta to serve 4 people

Freshly grated Parmesan cheese

1. Gently sauté onion in olive oil 1 minute. Add carrot and celery and cook for another 2 minutes. Do not allow vegetables to brown.

2. Add chopped tomatoes, salt and pepper and bring to a boil. Simmer 20-30 minutes until the sauce has thickened.

3. Purée in a blender.

4. Spoon over pasta and serve with grated Parmesan cheese.

Makes 4 servings.

Each serving contains:

Cal	Prot	Carb	Fib	Tot. Fat	Sat. Fat	Chol	Sodium
284	9g	34g	3g	13g	3g	5mg	439mg

NEAPOLITAN TOMATO SAUCE

In the eighteenth century Naples became the Italian home of tomatoes from the New World. The cooks did not bother to peel the tomatoes, but they did remove the seeds before coarsely chopping them. It is only in recent times that tomatoes have been peeled for a tomato sauce.

2 cloves garlic, peeled and crushed

1/4 cup (60ml) olive oil

2 lb. (900g) very ripe tomatoes, coarsely chopped

Pinch of sugar

Salt and pepper to taste

Cooked pasta to serve 4 people

Freshly grated Parmesan cheese

Variations

1. If tomatoes are not quite ripe, add 1 tablespoon tomato purée or use two cans (20-oz. / 600g) of tomatoes instead. With the latter, continue cooking until liquid has evaporated.

2. Add 1 small peeled minced onion or 1 seeded minced green or red chile pepper with the garlic.

1. Gently sauté garlic in olive oil in a large saucepan. After 1-2 minutes add tomatoes, sugar, salt and pepper.

2. Bring to a boil and cook over medium heat for 10 to 15 minutes, stirring frequently. The tomatoes should cook down to a thick sauce. Use sauce as it is or purée in a blender.

3. Spoon sauce over pasta or toss together. Serve with freshly grated Parmesan cheese.

Makes 4 servings.

Each serving contains:

Cal	Prot	Carb	Fib	Tot. Fat	Sat. Fat	Chol	Sodium
318	9g	35g	3g	17g	3g	5mg	204mg

TUSCAN TOMATO-AND-BASIL SAUCE

Carrot gives an added sweetness to this traditionally robust sauce from Tuscany. Serve with a green salad dressed with ewe's-milk or goat's-milk ricotta and lemon juice.

1-1/2 lb. (700g) ripe tomatoes or 2 cans (14-oz. / 400g) tomatoes

1 small carrot, peeled and grated

Salt and pepper to taste

Leaves from 5-6 sprigs of basil, roughly chopped

Cooked pasta to serve 4 people

Freshly grated Parmesan cheese

1. Place tomatoes, carrot, salt and pepper in a saucepan. Bring to a boil, cover and cook over medium heat 15-20 minutes until fairly thick.

2. Purée in a blender. Add basil and spoon over the pasta. Serve with freshly grated Parmesan cheese.

Makes 4 servings.

Variations

1. Finely chop half a small onion and add with the grated carrot.

2. Instead of basil, flavor with a little grated lemon peel and the juice of 1 small orange.

Each serving contains:

Cal	Prot	Carb	Fib	Tot. Fat	Sat. Fat	Chol	Sodium
192	8g	34g	3g	3g	1g	5mg	205mg

MUSHROOM SAUCE

Like tomato sauce, this thick paste of cooked mushrooms will be found in every Italian cook's repertoire. It is particularly useful because any kind of mushroom can be used, even button mushrooms! I often make double or triple quantities and keep batches in the freezer to use in more-substantial sauces, such as Variation 2 (below).

2 cloves garlic, peeled and crushed
6-7 tablespoons olive oil or
   6 tablespoons (75g) butter
3/4 lb. (340g) mushrooms, minced
Salt and pepper to taste
Whipping cream or oil (optional)
Cooked pasta to serve 4 people

Variations

1. Cover 1/4 oz. (8g) dried mushrooms with boiling water; let stand 20 minutes. Mince with fresh mushrooms.

2. Prepare 4 Italian sausages as directed on page 92, skin and crumble meat. Mix with sauce, 2 tablespoons chopped fresh parsley and a little more olive oil.

1. Gently sauté garlic in oil or butter until it starts to color.

2. Add mushrooms, salt and pepper. Cook slowly until mixture softens and darkens; this may take up to 15 minutes. Take care that it does not burn.

3. Discard any liquid and add enough whipping cream or oil to make a thick sauce. Add pasta and toss together.

Makes 4 servings.

Each serving contains:

Cal	Prot	Carb	Fib	Tot. Fat	Sat. Fat	Chol	Sodium
352	6g	29g	2g	25g	3g	0mg	71mg

CREAM-AND-HERB SAUCE

A recipe for a simpler cream-and-herb sauce is given on page 11 of Extra-Quick Sauces. The extra effort required by this version is more than repaid by the added subtlety of flavor. Almost any herb can be used. In addition to the more-obvious herbs, try watercress, fennel, lemon balm or chervil. This sauce is delicious with delicate capelli d'angelo pasta. Follow it with fresh pears and almonds.

1/4 cup (60ml) well-flavored vegetable or chicken stock

1/2 cup (125ml) whipping cream

1/4 cup (50g) butter, cut into pieces

Salt and pepper to taste

Pinch of cayenne pepper

Pinch of grated nutmeg

4 oz. (115g) freshly grated Parmesan cheese (1 cup)

1/4 cup (60ml) chopped fresh herbs

Cooked pasta to serve 4 people

1. Place stock and cream in a saucepan and bring to a boil. Simmer over medium heat to reduce.
2. After 6-7 minutes, start beating in pieces of butter with a wooden spoon. When all the butter has been incorporated, stir in salt, pepper, cayenne and nutmeg.
3. Next add half the cheese, the herbs and the pasta. Toss well together and serve with remaining Parmesan cheese sprinkled over the top.

Makes 4 servings.

Each serving contains:

Cal	Prot	Carb	Fib	Tot. Fat	Sat. Fat	Chol	Sodium
457	17g	26g	1g	32g	20g	94mg	772mg

BROCCOLI-AND-PINE-NUT SAUCE

I came across this unusual sauce on the Italian coast south of Naples. It is both quick to make and attractive to look at. The flavors and textures are good too.

1/4 cup (60ml) olive oil

2 cloves garlic, peeled and crushed

3/4 cup (115g) breadcrumbs

Salt and pepper to taste

3/4 lb. (340g) broccoli, cut into florets

Cooked pasta to serve 4 people

2 tablespoons pine nuts, toasted (page xiv)

Extra-virgin olive oil

Freshly grated Parmesan cheese

Variations

1. Add 2 tablespoons sesame seeds to the breadcrumbs and omit garlic and pine nuts. Serve with roasted sesame oil mixed with olive oil.

2. Add a 2-oz. (60g) can of anchovies, drained and chopped, to the breadcrumb mixture and omit garlic and Parmesan cheese.

1. Heat oil in a large skillet and sauté the garlic for 1 minute. Add breadcrumbs, salt and pepper and sauté until crisp and golden.

2. Cook broccoli in a little salted boiling water or steam until tender. Do not overcook.

3. Divide pasta among 4 plates and sprinkle with breadcrumbs. Top with broccoli and toasted pine nuts.

4. Serve with extra-virgin olive oil and freshly grated Parmesan cheese.

Makes 4 servings.

Each serving contains:

Cal	Prot	Carb	Fib	Tot. Fat	Sat. Fat	Chol	Sodium
464	13g	44g	5g	28g	5g	5mg	369mg

LEBANESE LENTIL SAUCE

I have never really thought of the Middle East as a pasta-eating area but a Lebanese friend of mine often serves noodles with her main-course dishes. Lentils, on the other hand, are very much a part of the Lebanese tradition and are often served mixed with rice. She tells me that this recipe is supposed to be older than Marco Polo, but where the pasta came from in those days is anybody's guess.

1/4 lb. (115g) whole green lentils, washed

1/4 cup (60ml) olive oil

1 large onion, peeled and minced

1 large clove garlic, peeled and minced

Salt and pepper to taste

2 tablespoons chopped fresh cilantro or coriander leaves

Cooked pasta to serve 4 people

Olive oil

Fresh cilantro or coriander sprigs

1. Cover lentils with plenty of water and bring to a boil. Simmer 20-25 minutes until just tender. Do not allow them to become mushy.

2. Heat 1/4 cup oil in another pan and sauté onion and garlic until they are golden brown. Add drained lentils, salt, pepper and cilantro or coriander and mix carefully together.

3. Add a little olive oil to the pasta. Spoon lentil sauce over pasta and garnish with fresh cilantro or coriander.

Makes 4 servings.

Each serving contains:

Cal	Prot	Carb	Fib	Tot. Fat	Sat. Fat	Chol	Sodium
295	7g	34g	3g	15g	2g	0mg	72mg

SICILIAN PEPPER SAUCE

Capers and olives are typical ingredients in sun-drenched Sicily. I've added succulent sweet peppers and onions. Serve this sauce with long thin pasta such as vermicelli or capelli d'angelo, and mop up the juices with a warm ciabatta roll.

4 large bell peppers of mixed colors, quartered and seeded

2 large onions, peeled and sliced

2 cloves garlic, peeled and chopped

5 tablespoons extra-virgin olive oil

1 tablespoon red wine vinegar

1 teaspoon tomato purée

2 tablespoons water

6 large green olives, pitted and chopped

1 tablespoon capers, drained

Salt and pepper to taste

Pinch of dried oregano

Cooked pasta to serve 4 people

Freshly grated Parmesan cheese

1. Grill peppers or char over an open flame. Peel and cut into strips.

2. Sauté onion and garlic in the olive oil for 4-5 minutes until lightly browned.

3. Add remaining sauce ingredients and bring to a boil. Cook over medium heat 10 minutes, stirring occasionally. Spoon onto the pasta and serve with freshly grated cheese.

Makes 4 servings.

Variation

Add 3-4 anchovy fillets, well chopped, or 2 teaspoons anchovy paste (page 36). Serve with chopped parsley rather than Parmesan cheese.

Each serving contains:

Cal	Prot	Carb	Fib	Tot. Fat	Sat. Fat	Chol	Sodium
357	8g	37g	4g	20g	4g	5mg	412mg

PROVENÇALE SAUCE

In some ways the food of Provence is as Italian as Italy itself. Traditional dishes such as Pissaladiere and Soupe au Pistou are very similar to Italian specialties like Pizza and Pesto Sauce. At one time the coastal areas of Provence were part of the Italian province of Liguria.

The Italian influences are still very strong. This is a typical Provence-style sauce for pasta. It has a tendency to splash when it is boiling so use a very deep pan, but do not cover with a lid. Being oil-based, this sauce goes well with any kind of long pasta. I like it particularly with vermicelli.

2 large cloves garlic, peeled and chopped

1 medium onion, peeled and minced

2 tablespoons olive oil

1 can (14-oz. / 400g) can tomatoes

1 oz. (25g) small black olives (8-10 olives)

1 teaspoon large Italian capers

Salt and pepper to taste

2 large sprigs basil, roughly torn

Cooked pasta to serve 4 people

1. Sauté garlic and onion in the oil for 4-5 minutes until lightly browned.
2. Add tomatoes, olives, capers, salt and pepper and bring to a boil. Boil rapidly for 15 minutes, stirring occasionally to prevent the sauce from sticking to the pan.
3. Just before serving add basil and toss with the pasta.

Makes 4 servings.

Each serving contains:

Cal	Prot	Carb	Fib	Tot. Fat	Sat. Fat	Chol	Sodium
221	5g	32g	3g	8g	1g	0mg	326mg

ASPARAGUS TIPS WITH LEMON GRASS

Pasta, they say, was invented in the East so I have combined some of the flavors of Thai and Malaysian cooking with fresh spring vegetables to make a very attractive dish. Keep the vegetables slightly crunchy and arrange the plates with care.

3 short sticks lemon grass

3 cloves garlic, peeled and halved

2 small pieces fresh ginger, peeled

6 tablespoons peanut oil

12 baby corn, halved lengthwise

1 lb. (450g) asparagus, cut into 2-1/2-inch (6cm) lengths

1/4 lb. (115g) sugar peas, cut in half lengthwise

Juice of 2 oranges

1/4 teaspoon ground coriander

Cooked pasta to serve 4 people

1/4 cup (60ml) shredded coconut, toasted

1. To flavor oil, gently cook lemon grass, garlic and ginger in oil 2-3 minutes, taking care not to let it get too hot. Remove seasonings from oil and discard.

2. Boil corn in salted water about 5 minutes.

3. Reheat flavored oil and add corn, asparagus and sugar peas. Toss vegetables until they are well coated. Add orange juice and coriander and bring to a boil. Simmer 5 minutes until asparagus is tender.

4. Add pasta and toss well together.

5. Spoon onto 4 plates, pouring juices over the top; sprinkle with toasted coconut.

Makes 4 servings.

Each serving contains:

Cal	Prot	Carb	Fib	Tot. Fat	Sat. Fat	Chol	Sodium
402	9g	42g	6g	24g	5g	0mg	28mg

ITALIAN SALSA VERDE

This pretty green sauce and its more-piquant cousin *Salsa Picante* do not need cooking but they can be gently heated to keep the pasta from getting cold too quickly. Be careful not to overheat them. Both can be made in a food processor or blender. The flavor remains as good but the texture disappears, leaving a fairly smooth and creamy sauce.

Both sauces improve with keeping. I often make double quantities and store half in the refrigerator to use later in the week. They are both served as starters, as it is difficult to keep larger quantities of pasta hot.

1 mixed bunch of fresh parsley and basil, minced

2 small celery stalks, trimmed and chopped

1/2 small onion, peeled and chopped

1 tablespoon capers, roughly chopped

2 hard-cooked egg yolks, minced

2 teaspoons lemon juice

6 tablespoons olive oil

Salt and pepper to taste

Cooked pasta to serve 4 people as a starter

1. Combine parsley, basil, celery, onion, capers and egg yolks.
2. Stir in lemon juice and oil to form a thick sauce.
3. Place in a small saucepan with salt and pepper and heat very gently. Spoon over the pasta and serve at once.

Makes 4 servings.

Each serving contains:

Cal	Prot	Carb	Fib	Tot. Fat	Sat. Fat	Chol	Sodium
301	5g	19g	2g	23g	4g	106mg	189mg

SALSA PICANTE

I like this made with cornichons, or small French gherkins, but any kind of pickle will do.

1 hard-cooked egg, minced

5-6 anchovy fillets, drained and minced

3 tablespoons chopped fresh parsley

3 tablespoons pickle, minced

2 tablespoons capers, minced

1 clove garlic, peeled and crushed

1 tablespoon lemon juice

6 tablespoons extra-virgin olive oil

1/4 teaspoon cayenne pepper

Salt and pepper to taste

Cooked pasta to serve 4 people as a starter

1. Combine all chopped and minced ingredients, then add lemon juice, oil, cayenne pepper, salt and pepper.
2. Place in a small saucepan and heat very gently. Spoon over the pasta and serve at once.

Makes 4 servings.

Each serving contains:

Cal	Prot	Carb	Fib	Tot. Fat	Sat. Fat	Chol	Sodium
301	6g	19g	1g	22g	3g	58mg	510mg

Anchovies ~ *These strongly flavored little fish can be bought packed in oil or brine. Soak the latter in water to remove some of the salt. You can tone down the flavor of anchovies by soaking them in milk before using. Discard the soaking liquid.*

You can now buy small jars of Italian anchovy paste. This has a very soft texture and is ideal for sauces. Use 2-3 tablespoons for a strength of flavor equivalent to a small can (2-oz. / 50g) of anchovies.

MARINARA SAUCES

Marinara is the Italian word meaning *of the sea*. It is a useful collective term for the many tuna-based sauces that are popular in Italy. Like all fish-based sauces they are usually *not* served with cheese.

TUNA SAUCE

This is the simplest of all the tuna-based sauces. It is popular all over Southern Italy where it is usually served with spaghetti and garnished with a handful of small black olives and a wedge of lemon. Add a basket of hearty country bread and spoon any extra sauce over bread chunks if you are still hungry! Use tuna canned in oil, not water.

1 can (7-oz. / 200g) tuna in oil

2 tablespoons extra-virgin olive oil

3 tablespoons chopped fresh parsley

1/2 cup (125ml) chicken stock

Salt and pepper to taste

Cooked pasta to serve 4 people

1. Empty tuna and its oil into a saucepan. Mash with a fork and add olive oil. Cook gently for 5 minutes.
2. Add parsley, chicken stock, salt and pepper and cook for 5 minutes.
3. Spoon over the pasta or toss together and serve at once with more black pepper.

Makes 4 servings.

Each serving contains:

Cal	Prot	Carb	Fib	Tot. Fat	Sat. Fat	Chol	Sodium
278	18g	24g	1g	12g	2g	15mg	362mg

TUNA-AND-TOMATO SAUCE

This is a more-substantial recipe I picked up near Amalfi. The sauce was the specialty of a little restaurant perched high on the steep hillside overlooking the port. I chose the dish as a main course with a crisp green salad on the side.

1 can (7-oz. / 200g) tuna in oil
2 tablespoons olive oil
2 onions, peeled and minced
1 clove garlic, peeled and crushed
1/4 teaspoon dried oregano
2 teaspoons tomato purée
1 can (8-oz. / 225g) tomatoes
Salt and pepper to taste
2 tablespoons chopped fresh basil
1 tablespoon chopped fresh parsley
Cooked pasta to serve 4 people

1. Drain oil from the tuna into a pan, add the olive oil and sauté onions and garlic for 4-5 minutes until they turn light gold.

2. Add oregano, tomato purée and tomatoes. Bring to a boil, add salt and pepper and cook for 15 minutes, stirring occasionally.

3. Flake tuna into mixture and cook 5 minutes longer. Stir in fresh herbs, spoon over pasta and serve at once.

Makes 4 servings.

Variations

1. Omit basil. Add 3-4 anchovies and cook with the garlic and onions. This gives an even punchier flavor.

2. Instead of tuna use fresh or canned baby clams to make a Vongole Sauce, page 40.

Each serving contains:

Cal	Prot	Carb	Fib	Tot. Fat	Sat. Fat	Chol	Sodium
313	20g	32g	3g	12g	2g	9mg	348mg

TUNA WITH SHRIMP

This is a richer and slightly more-elegant variation on the tuna theme. For the best effect try to keep the tuna in definite flakes. This sauce is good with pasta shells as well as long pasta. Serve with a salad of mixed greens, shredded peppers and grated carrot.

2 tablespoons (25g) butter

1/4 lb. (115g) cooked peeled shrimp

Grated peel of 1/2 lemon

2 tablespoons chopped fresh parsley

Cooked pasta to serve 4 people

1 cup (250ml) whipping cream

Salt and pepper to taste

1 can (7-oz. / 200g) tuna in water, well drained and carefully flaked

1. Heat butter in a very large pan. Toss shrimp, lemon peel and parsley in the butter for a minute to heat through.

2. Add pasta, cream, salt and pepper and toss again over medium heat.

3. Carefully add the flaked tuna and serve immediately.

Makes 4 servings.

Each serving contains:

Cal	Prot	Carb	Fib	Tot. Fat	Sat. Fat	Chol	Sodium
462	24g	26g	1g	29g	18g	167mg	381mg

VONGOLE SAUCE

This seaside classic takes its name from the Italian word *vongola* or clam. Today mussels are usually used as well as clams. Two kinds of clam are found in Italy. One is small with a yellow shell. The other is larger and better flavored; it is distinguished by a gray shell with a dark-blue line through the middle.

Naples is said to be the homeland of Spaghetti Vongole. Some aficionados prefer the sauce *bianco,* or without tomatoes.

3 lb. (1.4kg) clams or 1 lb. (450g) clams and 2 lb. (900g) mussels

2 cloves garlic, peeled and crushed

1/4 cup (60ml) olive oil

1-1/2 lb. (700g) ripe tomatoes, blanched, peeled and diced

Salt and pepper to taste

Cooked pasta to serve 4 people

2 tablespoons chopped fresh parsley

1. Wash shellfish thoroughly and remove beards from the mussels if using. Soak 5 minutes in cold salted water before using.

2. Place shellfish in a large pan and shake over low heat until shells open. Remove from heat and discard any unopened shells. Remove shellfish from the pan and take about half of them out of their shells.

3. Sauté garlic in the olive oil. Add tomatoes, salt and pepper and cook 10-15 minutes.

4. Add all shellfish and any juices. Stir to coat with sauce and heat through.

5. Toss pasta in this mixture and serve sprinkled with the parsley.

Makes 4 servings.

Each serving contains:

Cal	Prot	Carb	Fib	Tot. Fat	Sat. Fat	Chol	Sodium
306	11g	33g	3g	15g	2g	14mg	107mg

PUTTANESCA SAUCE

This gutsy sauce originated in the slums of Naples. Tradition has it that the recipe was dreamed up by the *puttanas,* or prostitutes, who ply their trade in narrow streets around the old port. Its piquant flavor is popular all over Italy.

1/4 cup (60ml) olive oil

2 tablespoons (25g) butter

2 cloves garlic, peeled and crushed

1 small fresh green chile pepper, seeded and minced

4 anchovy fillets, chopped

1 lb. (450g) ripe tomatoes, blanched, peeled and diced

1 tablespoon tomato purée

1/2 cup (125g) black olives, pitted and chopped

1 tablespoon capers

Cooked pasta to serve 4 people

2 tablespoons chopped fresh parsley

Freshly grated Parmesan cheese

1. Heat oil and butter in a saucepan and sauté garlic, chile pepper and anchovies 2-3 minutes.

2. Add tomatoes, tomato purée, olives and capers and cook 6-7 minutes, stirring constantly.

3. Spoon over the pasta. Sprinkle with parsley and serve with Parmesan cheese.

Makes 4 servings.

Each serving contains:

Cal	Prot	Carb	Fib	Tot. Fat	Sat. Fat	Chol	Sodium
379	9g	33g	3g	24g	7g	24mg	577mg

CRAB-AND-GINGER SAUCE

Good-quality white crabmeat is essential for this exotic starter. The flavors are subtle but delicious. Serve with a delicate side salad of lamb's lettuce dressed with olive oil and a dash of orange juice.

1 can (7-oz. / 200g) white crabmeat

1/4 cup (50g) butter

3-4 green onions, trimmed and chopped

1 piece (1-in. / 2.5cm) fresh ginger, peeled and grated

1 cup (250ml) whipping cream

1/4 cup (60ml) white wine

Salt and pepper to taste

Cooked pasta to serve 4 people, as a starter

Variation

This dish is very attractive garnished with small mounds of red lumpfish caviar or, for a special occasion, the juicier keta or salmon caviar.

1. Drain crabmeat and tip onto a plate. Pick over carefully to remove any membrane and bits of shell.
2. Melt butter in a large saucepan and gently sauté onions and ginger for 2-3 minutes, being careful not to brown them.
3. Add cream, wine, salt and pepper. Bring mixture to a boil and cook 4-5 minutes to thicken the sauce.
4. Stir in the crabmeat and heat through. Add pasta and toss. Serve with black pepper.

Makes 4 servings.

Each serving contains:

Cal	Prot	Carb	Fib	Tot. Fat	Sat. Fat	Chol	Sodium
457	15g	20g	1g	35g	21g	157mg	377mg

VENETIAN FISH-AND-FENNEL SAUCE

Whether you are lazing by the Lido in Venice or tramping the hills of Verona you are sure to come across bigoli. It is one of the principal types of local pasta in the Veneto. It is usually served with a simple anchovy-and-garlic sauce such as that found on page 3 but can also be served with sardines. I added fennel and the result was excellent.

Ask the butcher to prepare the fish for you.

2 cloves garlic, peeled and crushed

4 tablespoons chopped fresh fennel or 1/4 teaspoon fennel seeds

2 tablespoons chopped fresh parsley

6 tablespoons olive oil

8 large sardines or sprats, filleted

Freshly ground black pepper

Cooked pasta to serve 4 people

2 tablespoons lemon juice

2 tablespoons pine nuts, toasted (page xiv)

1. Sauté garlic and herbs in oil for 1 minute. Add sardines or sprats. Cook 2 minutes on each side and season with pepper.
2. Toss pasta in a little more oil and spoon onto 4 plates. Arrange sardines or sprats on top.
3. Add lemon juice to the pan. Bring to a boil and pour over the sardines.
4. Garnish with the toasted pine nuts and serve at once.

Makes 4 servings.

Each serving contains:

Cal	Prot	Carb	Fib	Tot. Fat	Sat. Fat	Chol	Sodium
391	12g	27g	2g	27g	4g	34mg	126mg

SOLE WITH CAPERS AND BALSAMIC VINEGAR

Sole is plentiful along the Tuscan coast and this recipe comes from a restaurant in the bustling port of Livorno. It is dressed with balsamic vinegar from neighboring Emilia Romagna. The result is rich and fruity.

1 carrot, peeled and sliced

1 onion, peeled and sliced

1 bay leaf

Salt and pepper to taste

1/2 cup (125ml) water

2 Dover sole, filleted

6 tablespoons extra-virgin olive oil

Cooked pasta to serve 4 people

2 tablespoons capers, drained and washed

2 teaspoons balsamic vinegar

1. In a deep skillet combine carrot, onion, bay leaf, salt, pepper and water. Simmer 10 minutes.
2. Cut sole into strips and add to liquid. Poach over low heat 2-3 minutes until cooked.
3. Drain the liquid. Keep fish warm while you heat oil very gently in another saucepan.
4. Add half the oil to pasta, toss and spoon onto 4 plates. Top with fish and capers and sprinkle with vinegar and remaining oil. Serve at once with more black pepper.

Makes 4 servings.

Each serving contains:

Cal	Prot	Carb	Fib	Tot. Fat	Sat. Fat	Chol	Sodium
393	20g	29g	2g	22g	3g	39mg	299mg

MEXICAN SHRIMP-AND-ONION SAUCE

The taste of this Mexican specialty with its lime juice and cayenne pepper is quite different from the traditional flavors of Italy but it works extremely well with pasta. I usually serve it with spaghettini as an elegant starter. It tastes just as good hot, warm or even cold.

2 onions, peeled and thinly sliced
Juice and grated peel of 1 lime
1 tablespoon extra-virgin olive oil
1 clove garlic, peeled and crushed
2 tablespoons white wine vinegar
Pinch of dried oregano
Salt and pepper to taste
Pinch of cayenne or hot paprika
20 large cooked, peeled shrimp
Cooked pasta to serve 4 people
*   as a starter*

1. Marinate onions and lime peel in the lime juice for as long as you have time.
2. Pour marinating liquid off the onions and set aside.
3. Heat oil in a skillet and sauté garlic for 1 minute. Remove from the heat and add onions. Stir and return to the heat. Cook 2 minutes, stirring constantly.
4. Add remaining ingredients except shrimp and pasta. Bring to a boil; add shrimp and marinade and toss well together.
5. Spoon over the pasta. Add more oil and toss well. Serve with more black pepper.

Makes 4 servings.

Each serving contains:

Cal	Prot	Carb	Fib	Tot. Fat	Sat. Fat	Chol	Sodium
166	10g	22g	2g	4g	1g	59mg	136mg

ITALIAN MEAT SAUCE

Italy has many meat-based pasta sauces, but Bolognese is the most famous and the only one to have been standardized. The official recipe, kept by the Bologna Chamber of Commerce, requires lean ground veal, onion, tomatoes, lemon zest, nutmeg, and celery, carrot and prosciutto fried in butter. A dash of cream is added at the end.

EVERYDAY MEAT SAUCE

If you do not have all the ingredients on hand for Classic Bolognese Sauce (page 47), here is a simple but tasty meat sauce for spaghetti. For variety, add 1/2 cup minced button mushrooms.

2 slices bacon, diced (optional)

2 tablespoons olive oil

2 cloves garlic, peeled and minced

1 onion, peeled and minced

1 lb. (450g) lean ground beef

2 tablespoons tomato purée

1/4 teaspoon dried oregano or wild marjoram

Salt and pepper to taste

Pinch of grated nutmeg (optional)

1 can (14-oz. / 400g) tomatoes

1/4 cup (60ml) red wine or beef stock

Cooked pasta to serve 4 people

1. Sauté diced bacon, if using, in the oil and add garlic and onion. Brown lightly.

2. Add ground beef and cook for 3-4 minutes until lightly browned.

3. Add remaining sauce ingredients and bring to a boil. Simmer, uncovered, for 20 minutes, stirring occasionally.

4. Toss pasta in sauce and serve.

Makes 4 servings.

Each serving contains:

Cal	Prot	Carb	Fib	Tot. Fat	Sat. Fat	Chol	Sodium
555	39g	32g	3g	28g	9g	112mg	342mg

CLASSIC BOLOGNESE SAUCE

In Bologna this sauce is used mainly in lasagne, but in the rest of Italy and throughout the world it is most often used with spaghetti. All Italian cooks have their own variations of the recipe but all agree that the original was cooked in an earthenware pot for as long as possible. My version can be cooked in 30 minutes.

Unsmoked pancetta or unsmoked bacon can be used in place of prosciutto crudo. Sauté it in the butter before adding the vegetables.

2 tablespoons (25g) butter

1 onion, peeled and minced

1 small carrot, peeled and minced

2 celery stalks, minced

3 oz. (85g) prosciutto crudo, diced

1 lb. (450g) lean ground beef

1/2 cup (125ml) red wine

1-1/2 tablespoons tomato purée

1/4 cup (60ml) water

1/4 teaspoon grated lemon peel

Pinch of grated nutmeg

Salt and pepper to taste

2 tablespoons whipping cream

Cooked pasta to serve 4 people

Butter

Freshly grated Parmesan cheese

1. Melt butter in a pan and gently sauté onion, carrot and celery for 3-4 minutes. Add prosciutto and cook another minute or so.

2. Stir in the ground beef and brown. Add remaining sauce ingredients except cream. Bring to a boil, reduce heat and simmer, uncovered, 30 minutes.

3. Stir in cream and toss pasta in sauce. Top with a pat of butter and serve with grated Parmesan cheese.

Makes 4 servings.

Each serving contains:

Cal	Prot	Carb	Fib	Tot. Fat	Sat. Fat	Chol	Sodium
629	45g	31g	2g	33g	15g	153mg	679mg

CHICKEN LIVERS WITH LEEKS AND RED WINE

Charbroiled peppers and chicken livers are arranged in an attractive pattern on top of the pasta. I like this sauce with spaghettini. Serve with a bowl of lightly cooked warm spinach leaves tossed in lemon juice.

2 red bell peppers, quartered and seeded

2 large leeks, trimmed and cut into 2-1/2-inch (6cm) lengths

2 tablespoons olive oil

12 chicken livers

Salt and pepper to taste

1/2 cup (125ml) condensed beef stock

3 tablespoons red wine

Cooked pasta to serve 4 people

A few sprigs of fresh chervil

1. Broil peppers skin-side up until well charred. Place in a bowl and cover for 10-15 minutes. Remove skin and cut peppers into long thin strips. Keep warm.

2. Steam leeks over boiling, salted water. Cut into long thin strips and keep warm.

3. Heat oil in a pan. Season chicken livers with salt and pepper, then sauté. Cook until pink in the middle, remove from pan and keep warm.

4. Pour stock and wine into the pan and bring to a boil, stirring constantly. Boil mixture 3-4 minutes to reduce. Add salt and pepper.

5. Place pasta on 4 plates. Cut chicken livers in half and arrange around pasta.

6. Sprinkle leeks over the top and arrange pepper strips in center.

7. Pour juices over each serving and garnish with chervil. Serve at once.

Makes 4 servings.

Each serving contains:

Cal	Prot	Carb	Fib	Tot. Fat	Sat. Fat	Chol	Sodium
334	21g	36g	3g	11g	2g	379mg	319mg

SUN-DRIED-TOMATO-AND-RED-PEPPER SAUCE

Mediterranean cooks have found that grilling peppers makes them sweeter and more aromatic. The charred taste of any remaining skin adds to the flavor.

1 oz. (25g) sun-dried tomatoes

2-3 red bell peppers, quartered and seeded

1/4 cup (60ml) extra-virgin olive oil

1 onion, peeled and sliced

Salt and pepper to taste

Cooked pasta to serve 4 people

Aged Pecorino cheese, grated

1. Soak sun-dried tomatoes in boiling water to soften; cut into thin strips.

2. Broil peppers skin-side up until well charred. Remove from heat and let stand 10 minutes. Peel and cut into strips.

3. Heat oil in a skillet and sauté onion until it starts to brown. Add tomatoes, red bell peppers, salt and pepper. Toss together over medium heat.

4. Place pasta on 4 serving plates. Top with tomato-pepper mixture, and serve with more olive oil and Pecorino cheese.

Makes 4 servings.

Each serving contains:

Cal	Prot	Carb	Fib	Tot. Fat	Sat. Fat	Chol	Sodium
311	8g	34g	3g	16g	3g	5mg	334mg

Sun-Dried Tomatoes ~ *You can buy these strongly flavored dried tomatoes loose or packed in oil. The former need to be soaked in boiling water before use. Sun-dried tomatoes can also be bought puréed—a teaspoonful of this paste will jazz up all kinds of tomato and meat-based sauces.*

Chapter Three

LONG FLAT PASTA

Long flat pasta ranges from wide noodles with fluted edges, through the popular tagliatelle, to the much-finer linguine. It is often, but not always, made with egg and may be flavored with spinach to produce green pasta or tomato to give pale-pink pasta.

This pasta is traditionally served with thicker cream sauces, cheese or eggs. The Italians also serve tagliatelle with meat-based sauces.

All types of pasta listed below are available dried and some are sold fresh. A few are made with whole-wheat flour.

For cooking instructions, see page xiii.

TAGLIATELLE—The classic egg noodle of Emilia Romagna has traveled the world in various forms. For centuries the exact width of tagliatelle was argued over, but in 1972 a gastronomic law was passed in Italy whereby a strand of tagliatelle has to measure 8mm (1/3 inch) across when cooked. Any pasta not conforming to this measurement must be sold under another name.

Tagliatelle may be packed in straight medium-sized lengths or in curled bundles or nests and it may be plain or flavored. Like spaghetti it is extremely versatile and can be used with most of the quick sauces in Chapter 1.

NOODLES—This is the general term often given to tagliatelle-like pasta which does not conform to the correct measurement.

PAPPARDELLE—A very wide tagliatelle often served in Tuscany. Usually home-made, it can occasionally be bought ready-made.

FETTUCCINE—The Roman version of tagliatelle is traditionally made a little narrower and a little thicker. In the Veneto this type of pasta is called *paparele*.

LINGUINE—Linguine is also known as *bavette* in Tuscany. It is much thinner than tagliatelle, being only about 1/8 inch (3mm) wide. It needs a more-delicate sauce or it will be swamped. It is also used in soups and soufflés. *Tagliolini* is a home-made version.

TRENETTE—Falling somewhere between tagliatelle and linguine, this Ligurian specialty is the pasta to partner pesto sauce (pages 58-60). It can also be used with any of the quick sauces in Chapter 1. Not content with adding plenty of herbs to their sauces, the Ligurians also add fresh herbs to trenette dough to make the speckled *trenette verde*.

LASAGNETTE—Popular in Southern Italy in Calabria, this long dried pasta is about 3/4 inch (2cm) wide, with attractive curly edges. It is served with fairly robust, often meat-based, sauces. The straight-edged variety is known as *lasagne*.

FRESH CHEESE-AND-TOMATO SAUCE

The fresh flavors of this virtually uncooked sauce are delicious in the summer sunshine. Serve as a starter with linguine or double to make a substantial main course with a salad of sliced peppers, black olives and cucumber.

1/4 (60ml) cup extra-virgin olive oil

4 green onions, minced

8 oz. (225g) ricotta cheese (1 cup)

4 medium tomatoes, diced

Leaves from 6 large sprigs of basil, roughly torn

Salt and pepper to taste

Cooked pasta to serve 4 people as a starter

1. Gently heat oil in a pan and add onions and ricotta. After 1 minute stir in the tomatoes, basil, salt and pepper.
2. Remove from heat as soon as mixture is warmed through. Toss with pasta and serve.

Makes 4 servings.

Variation

Use fresh goat cheese in place of ricotta cheese.

Each serving contains:

Cal	Prot	Carb	Fib	Tot. Fat	Sat. Fat	Chol	Sodium
343	10g	24g	2g	23g	7g	29mg	128mg

Ricotta Cheese ~ *Ricotta is known as cheese but is in fact a byproduct of cheese-making. It is made from the whey left after the curds have been made into cheese. Cow's-milk ricotta is very crumbly; ewe's-milk ricotta is much creamier. Both have a delicate fresh flavor.*

EAST-WEST SAUCE

This California recipe mixes the flavors of East and West with excellent results. It is best served with trenette. Finish the meal with a mixture of tropical fruits.

5 tablespoons peanut oil

1 tablespoon sesame oil

1 whole dried red chile pepper

1/2 lb. (225g) broccoli florets

1/4 lb. (115g) sugar peas

1 red bell pepper, seeded and diced

3 tablespoons soy sauce

3 tablespoons rice vinegar or white wine vinegar

Cooked pasta to serve 4 people

3 eggs, beaten

Fresh cilantro or coriander sprigs

1. Heat oils in a large pan. Sauté chile pepper 1 minute, then remove from pan and discard.

2. Toss vegetables into the oil and stir-fry 2-3 minutes.

3. Add soy sauce and vinegar and bring to a boil. Add pasta and toss together. Add eggs and toss again.

4. Serve garnished with sprigs of fresh cilantro or coriander.

Makes 4 servings.

Variations

1. Add a few drops of Tabasco Sauce for a hotter result.

2. Add grated peel and juice of 1 orange with the soy sauce and vinegar.

Each serving contains:

Cal	Prot	Carb	Fib	Tot. Fat	Sat. Fat	Chol	Sodium
396	12g	32g	4g	25g	5g	159mg	837mg

TUSCAN LIMA-BEAN SAUCE

Beans are a great favorite in Tuscany, where this sauce would be served with wide noodles or pappardelle. In Tuscany only fresh beans are used. Small frozen beans can be substituted, but you should remove their skins.

3/4 lb. (340g) fresh or frozen lima beans

3-4 shallots or 1 small onion, peeled and minced

1 stalk celery, trimmed and minced

2 tablespoons (25g) butter

3/4 cup (185ml) whipping cream

1/4 cup (60ml) condensed vegetable or chicken stock

Salt and pepper to taste

3 tablespoons chopped fresh parsley

Cooked pasta to serve 4 people

1. Cover beans with water and bring to a boil. Drain and, if necessary, slip off the skins.
2. Sauté shallots or onion and celery in butter 3-4 minutes.
3. Add prepared beans, cream and stock and bring to a boil. Simmer 5 minutes. Stir in salt, pepper and parsley and pour over the pasta. Serve at once.

Makes 4 servings.

Variations

1. For a less-rich sauce, substitute olive oil for butter and omit cream. Use 3/4 cup (185ml) stock and add 1 teaspoon cornstarch.
2. In winter Tuscans add a handful of wild mushrooms at the last minute.

Each serving contains:

Cal	Prot	Carb	Fib	Tot. Fat	Sat. Fat	Chol	Sodium
435	12g	45g	6g	24g	14g	77mg	249mg

FRESH-BEAN-AND-TOMATO SAUCE

Tiny fresh green beans are mixed with fresh lima beans to give an attractive appearance to this simple tagliatelle sauce from San Gimignano in the heart of Tuscany. From the restaurants in the main square you can see two of the seven distinctive towers of this famous walled hill town. The towers were built by successful citizens to show off their wealth.

1/2 lb. (225g) fresh or frozen lima beans

1/2 lb. (225g) fresh green beans, trimmed and cut into long thin strips

1/2 recipe Tuscan Tomato-and-Basil Sauce (page 27)

3 tablespoons whipping cream (optional)

Cooked pasta to serve 4 people

Freshly grated Parmesan cheese

Freshly ground black pepper

1. Blanch lima beans in boiling water for 3 minutes and slip off skins if necessary.
2. Return to the pan with green beans and cook another 5-6 minutes until tender.
3. Heat Tuscan Tomato-and-Basil Sauce in a large saucepan. Add cream, if using, and drained beans. Heat through again.
4. Add pasta and toss well together. Serve with Parmesan cheese and black pepper.

Makes 4 servings.

Each serving contains:

Cal	Prot	Carb	Fib	Tot. Fat	Sat. Fat	Chol	Sodium
326	16g	57g	8g	4g	1g	7mg	227mg

SAUTÉED MUSHROOMS WITH BALSAMIC VINEGAR

I first had this simple dish in a restaurant in the Piazza Fiore not far from the Tiber in Rome. Piles of fresh porcini decorated a side table and I discovered how large these mushrooms can be.

I like a mixture of large cultivated mushrooms for texture and dried wild mushrooms for flavor. Serve with wide, flat noodles and a green salad.

1 oz. (25g) dried mixed wild mushrooms

1 clove garlic, peeled and crushed

1/4 cup (60ml) chopped fresh parsley

1/4 cup (60ml) olive oil

1/2 lb. (225g) large fresh mushrooms, halved and sliced

1/2 teaspoon balsamic vinegar

Salt and pepper to taste

Cooked pasta to serve 4 people as a starter

1. Cover dried mushrooms with boiling water. Let stand 15-20 minutes. Drain, reserving liquid.
2. Gently sauté garlic and parsley in olive oil 1-2 minutes. Add both types of mushrooms. Continue cooking over medium heat, stirring frequently.
3. Mix balsamic vinegar with mushroom-soaking water and add to the pan. Season and toss over high heat for 1-2 minutes. Serve over pasta.

Makes 4 servings.

Each serving contains:

Cal	Prot	Carb	Fib	Tot. Fat	Sat. Fat	Chol	Sodium
241	6g	23g	3g	14g	2g	0mg	74mg

Balsamic Vinegar ~ *Genuine balsamic vinegar is produced only on private estates in Emilia Romagna and is expensive. It is made from unfermented grape juice and is aged for at least 12 years in a series of wooden casks. Commercial balsamic vinegar is not aged as long as the traditional vinegar, but a reasonably good version is still costly. The good news is that it has such an intense fruity flavor that you don't need to use very much.*

PESTO SAUCES

This Ligurian specialty is on the menu of every coastal restaurant from San Remo to Genoa. Each one offers its own variation of the classic sauce but what is essential is a large quantity of fresh basil. Pesto sauce can be served with almost any kind of long flat pasta.

Traditionally, sliced potatoes were cooked with the pasta and then both were drained and tossed in pesto sauce.

All three pesto sauces can be refrigerated for a week.

TUSCAN PESTO

In Tuscany, pine nuts are often replaced by walnuts to produce the region's own version of pesto sauce. It is usually served with spaghetti. Make sure you buy fresh walnuts for this dish. Any rancid flavors will be magnified once the sauce hits the hot pasta.

45-50 basil leaves (8-10 large sprigs)

3/4 cup (75g) walnuts

2 tablespoons (15g) freshly grated Parmesan cheese

6 tablespoons (75ml) extra-virgin olive oil

Salt and pepper to taste

Cooked pasta to serve 4 people

1. Place all sauce ingredients in a blender or food processor and blend for 1-2 minutes.

2. If sauce is too thick add a little more oil

3. Toss pasta in sauce over low heat and serve.

Makes 4 servings.

Each serving contains:

Cal	Prot	Carb	Fib	Tot. Fat	Sat. Fat	Chol	Sodium
451	9g	28g	2g	35g	5g	2mg	128mg

CLASSIC PESTO SAUCE

Here's the most-famous version.

45-50 basil leaves (8-10 large sprigs)

1/4 teaspoon salt

1-2 cloves garlic, peeled

2 tablespoons pine nuts

2 tablespoons (15g) freshly grated Parmesan cheese

1/4 cup (60ml) extra-virgin olive oil

Freshly ground black pepper

Cooked pasta to serve 4 people

1. Place all sauce ingredients in a blender or food processor and blend until smooth.
2. If sauce is too thick add a little more oil.
3. Toss pasta in the sauce over low heat and serve.

Makes 4 servings.

Variations

1. For a more-pungent flavor replace half the Parmesan cheese with Pecorino Sardo.
2. Toss 20 chopped black olives with the sauce and pasta.

Each serving contains:

Cal	Prot	Carb	Fib	Tot. Fat	Sat. Fat	Chol	Sodium
293	7g	26g	2g	19g	3g	2mg	193mg

CALIFORNIA PESTO SAUCE

Cilantro and *Chinese parsley* are names given to fresh coriander leaves, which are used to make a really pungent pesto sauce. You do not need to use many of them!

1 bunch of fresh cilantro or corian-der (approx. 1-1/2 oz. / 40g)

2 cloves garlic, peeled

2 tablespoons pine nuts

1 oz. (25g) freshly grated Parmesan cheese (1/4 cup)

1/4 cup (60ml) extra-virgin olive oil

Salt and pepper to taste

Cooked pasta to serve 4 people

1. Wash cilantro or coriander and dry on paper towels. Use stalks as well as leaves.

2. Place sauce ingredients in a blender or food processor and blend for 1-2 minutes.

3. If sauce is too thick add a little more oil.

4. Toss pasta in sauce over low heat and serve.

Makes 4 servings.

Each serving contains:

Cal	Prot	Carb	Fib	Tot. Fat	Sat. Fat	Chol	Sodium
312	9g	26g	2g	20g	4g	6mg	203mg

MUSHROOMS WITH WHISKEY

The inspiration for this dish comes from Scotland rather than Italy. It is the creation of an Edinburgh chef who has a passion for both wild mushrooms and his native brew. The rich and pungent sauce makes a great starter. It goes well with both linguine and spaghettini.

1 oz. (25g) dried mixed wild mushrooms

1 tablespoon whiskey

1 tablespoon (15g) butter

1 clove garlic, peeled and crushed

1 tablespoon chopped fresh parsley

1/4 cup (60ml) whipping cream

Cooked pasta to serve 4 people as a starter

Freshly ground black pepper

1. Cover mushrooms with boiling water. Let stand for 20 minutes. Add whiskey and steep another 30 minutes.

2. Melt butter in a skillet and lightly sauté garlic and parsley. Add mushrooms and soaking liquid to the pan.

3. Stir in whipping cream and bring to a boil. Continue cooking until sauce has thickened.

4. Mix thoroughly with pasta and serve with freshly ground black pepper.

Makes 4 servings.

Each serving contains:

Cal	Prot	Carb	Fib	Tot. Fat	Sat. Fat	Chol	Sodium
191	5g	20g	2g	9g	5g	28mg	39mg

Porcini ~ *Porcini are one of the popular wild mushrooms of Italy. They are very large and fleshy and have a distinctive earthy flavor. Packages of mixed wild mushrooms are available in most markets.*

GOLDEN SQUASH SAUCE

A side dish of steamed broccoli florets tossed in olive oil gives a good contrast of colors and textures to this beautiful golden sauce. Parmesan cheese is *not* served with this sauce.

3 cloves garlic, peeled and crushed

1 onion, peeled and minced

1 tablespoon olive oil

1 lb. (450g) banana, butternut or Hubbard squash, peeled, seeded and diced

1 cup (250ml) condensed vegetable stock

2 tablespoons chopped fresh parsley

1/2 cup (125ml) half-and-half

1/4 teaspoon grated nutmeg

Salt and pepper to taste

Cooked pasta to serve 4 people

1. Gently sauté garlic and onion in oil 3-4 minutes to soften.

2. Add squash and vegetable stock and bring to a boil. Cover and simmer 15 minutes, stirring occasionally, until squash is tender.

3. Mash with a wooden spoon and stir in parsley, half-and-half, nutmeg, salt and pepper. Cook a minute longer. If the sauce is too thick add a little pasta-cooking water. Pour sauce over pasta. Toss well together and serve at once.

Makes 4 servings.

Variation

Use whole garlic cloves and sauté with a chopped, seeded red chile pepper 2-3 minutes. Discard garlic and chile pepper and continue as above. For a *very* hot sauce include seeds of chile pepper.

Each serving contains:

Cal	Prot	Carb	Fib	Tot. Fat	Sat. Fat	Chol	Sodium
263	8g	42g	5g	8g	3g	11mg	93mg

ROMAN SAUCE

I first had this unusual pasta topping in a pretty restaurant nestled under the garden walls of the Villa d'Este in Rome. Swiss chard is eaten quite often in this city. Spinach could also be used but it tends to become soggy too quickly and its stalks do not give the same texture to the dish. This sauce is best served as a first course with fettuccine.

3/4 lb. (340g) Swiss chard, washed
1/4 cup (60ml) olive oil
1 clove garlic, peeled and chopped
2 tablespoons pine nuts
2 tablespoons raisins
Salt and pepper to taste
Cooked pasta to serve 4 people as
*   a starter*

Variation
  Use a little less oil and dress with 2-3 tablespoons whipping cream just before serving.

1. Cut stalks from chard and slice fairly thinly. Set aside.
2. Cook the leaves in a dry saucepan 3-4 minutes until just cooked. Squeeze dry and chop very roughly.
3. Heat oil in a skillet and sauté garlic for 1 minute. Add pine nuts and continue cooking until they begin to brown.
4. Toss sliced chard stalks into pan and stir-fry 2-3 minutes until they soften. Add chard leaves, raisins, salt and pepper, and toss over medium heat for about 2 minutes.
5. Spoon onto pasta and serve at once with more black pepper.

Makes 4 servings.

Each serving contains:

Cal	Prot	Carb	Fib	Tot. Fat	Sat. Fat	Chol	Sodium
267	6g	24g	3g	18g	2g	0mg	249mg

FRESH-SPINACH-AND-FETA-CHEESE SAUCE

This sauce can be served with any kind of noodle but it goes particularly well with broad flat noodles or lasagnette. Start the meal with grilled vegetables or a plate of Parma ham and melon.

1 large onion, peeled and very finely sliced

2 tablespoons olive oil

8-10 large leaves fresh spinach, shredded

10 oz. (300g) feta cheese, crumbled

6 tablespoons vegetable stock

Freshly ground black pepper

Cooked pasta to serve 4 people

1. Gently sauté onion in oil until soft but not brown.

2. Stir in spinach, feta cheese, stock and pepper and bring to a boil. Continue stirring until the cheese has begun to melt into the stock. The consistency should be creamy but lumpy.

3. Toss together with pasta and serve at once.

Makes 4 servings.

Each serving contains:

Cal	Prot	Carb	Fib	Tot. Fat	Sat. Fat	Chol	Sodium
402	18g	31g	2g	23g	14g	63mg	799mg

Vegetable Stock ~ *There are vegetable-stock cubes available that are not full of salt or monosodium glutamate but home-made stock is better. I keep all the cooking water from my vegetables and then, from time to time, boil it up with cooked vegetables such as carrot, onion and celery and any greens or herbs that are past their prime. Strain, taste and boil again if the flavor is not strong enough. A useful way to freeze stock is to pour it into ice-cube trays.*

PEASANT'S SAUCE

Every region of Italy has its own *paesana* or peasant's sauce. They are all vegetable-based and very quick and easy to make. I use any vegetables I have on hand so that some days it resembles the recipe exactly and other days it is like another dish.

It's fun to use a mixture of egg, spinach and tomato noodles or tagliatelle with this sauce. The rainbow effect is very attractive.

2 tablespoons cooking oil

1 onion, peeled and sliced

1 red bell pepper, seeded and thinly sliced

1 green bell pepper, seeded and thinly sliced

Salt and pepper to taste

Cooked pasta to serve 4 people

2 eggs, beaten

Freshly grated Parmesan cheese

Optional Extras

3 tablespoons frozen peas

3 tablespoons frozen corn

1/4 lb. (115g) button mushrooms, sliced or quartered

2-3 tomatoes, coarsely chopped

3 oz. (85g) chopped ham

1. Heat oil and sauté onion for 2 minutes until soft but not brown.

2. Add peppers, and any of the optional extras you wish. Continue cooking gently 5-6 minutes, stirring occasionally, until the vegetables have softened.

3. Season, add pasta and eggs and toss well over the heat. Serve at once with black pepper and Parmesan cheese.

Makes 4 servings.

Each serving contains:

Cal	Prot	Carb	Fib	Tot. Fat	Sat. Fat	Chol	Sodium
266	10g	29g	2g	12g	3g	111mg	217mg

CHINESE SAUCE

You can use Chinese egg noodles or Italian egg noodles with this Chinese-style stir-fried topping. You may substitute Greek Halloumi cheese for the tofu, but add the cheese at the very last minute or it will get too hard. Start the meal with spring rolls or shrimp toasts.

3 tablespoons peanut oil

2 teaspoons grated fresh ginger

2 cloves garlic, peeled and crushed

6-8 green onions, trimmed and sliced lengthwise

1 tablespoon cornstarch

Salt and pepper to taste

1/2 lb. (225g) tofu, cut into cubes

3 oz. (85g) sugar peas

1 green bell pepper, seeded and cut into strips

4 leaves Chinese cabbage

8 leaves Swiss chard, shredded

2 tablespoons cashew nuts, toasted (page xiv)

2 tablespoons light soy sauce

1/4 cup (60ml) vegetable stock

Cooked pasta to serve 4 people

Fresh parsley and chervil sprigs

1. Heat oil in a large wok or skillet. Add ginger, garlic and green onions and stir-fry for 1 minute.

2. Mix cornstarch, salt and pepper. Carefully toss tofu cubes in this mixture.

3. Add to the skillet and cook on all sides.

4. Add all the vegetables, nuts, soy sauce and stock and bring to a boil. Boil rapidly 1-2 minutes. Spoon over pasta and serve garnished with the sprigs of parsley and chervil.

Makes 4 servings.

Each serving contains:

Cal	Prot	Carb	Fib	Tot. Fat	Sat. Fat	Chol	Sodium
338	13g	39g	6g	16g	3g	0mg	807mg

TUNA-AND-WHITE-BEAN SAUCE

The inspiration for this filling sauce comes from a salad I had in Southern Spain. I liked the combination of flavors so much that I wanted to serve it as a hot dish as well as a cold salad. Here is the hot version I came up with. Serve it with wide noodles, accompanied by a simple mixed salad.

1/4 cup (60ml) olive oil

1 clove garlic, peeled and crushed

2 shallots or 4-5 green onions, trimmed and minced

1 bay leaf

6 oz. (175g) zucchini, diced

2 cans (7-oz. / 200g) tuna in water, drained and flaked

1 can (14-oz. / 400g) white kidney beans or cannellini beans, well drained

1 tablespoon capers

Salt and pepper to taste

Cooked pasta to serve 4 people

3 tablespoons chopped fresh parsley

1. Heat oil in a skillet and gently sauté garlic, shallots or green onions and bay leaf for 3-4 minutes. Do not allow the vegetables to brown. Remove bay leaf.

2. Add diced zucchini and toss over low heat for an additional 3-4 minutes.

3. Stir in remaining ingredients, except pasta and parsley, and heat over medium heat. Turn with a fork, being careful not to break up the tuna or mash the beans.

4. Serve spooned over the pasta with more olive oil on the side. Top with fresh parsley.

Makes 4 servings.

Each serving contains:

Cal	Prot	Carb	Fib	Tot. Fat	Sat. Fat	Chol	Sodium
523	35g	43g	6g	23g	4g	31mg	751mg

SALMON WITH WINE AND DILL

This special-occasion dish comes from the Silver Palate Restaurant in New York, where it is a firm favorite with the customers. It is quick to make and great for entertaining. For a memorable meal, serve with tagliatelle along with a side dish of sliced cucumber. Steamed fennel sprinkled with a little lemon juice also goes well with it.

1 cup (250ml) whipping cream
1/4 cup (50g) butter
1/4 cup (60ml) white wine
Salt and pepper to taste
Pinch of grated nutmeg
2 tablespoons (15g) freshly grated Parmesan cheese
1/4 cup (60ml) chopped fresh dill
3/4 lb. (340g) cooked fresh salmon, flaked
Cooked spinach pasta to serve 4 people
Fresh dill sprigs

1. Pour cream into a saucepan; add butter, wine, salt, pepper and nutmeg. Bring to a boil and cook until it is reduced by about a third.
2. Stir in cheese and dill. Carefully fold in the salmon.
3. Arrange pasta on 4 plates and top with the salmon-cream sauce. Garnish with sprigs of fresh dill.

Makes 4 servings.

Variation

Use 3 tablespoons sweet Martini or Cinzano Bianco in place of white wine.

Each serving contains:

Cal	Prot	Carb	Fib	Tot. Fat	Sat. Fat	Chol	Sodium
550	24g	26g	1g	38g	22g	159mg	323mg

SOLE IN TOMATO SAUCE

This well-flavored sauce comes from Brindisi on the Adriatic coast of Italy. The basic tomato sauce is packed with anchovies, olives and extra garlic. It is usually made with sole or monkfish.

1/4 cup (60ml) olive oil

1-2 cloves garlic, peeled and crushed

4 anchovy fillets, drained and chopped

1/2 recipe Neapolitan Tomato Sauce (page 26)

12 black olives, pitted, halved

Freshly ground black pepper

2 lemon sole, filleted and skinned

Cooked pasta to serve 4 people

4 teaspoons sour cream

1. Heat oil in a deep skillet and add garlic and anchovies. Sauté 1-2 minutes, stirring constantly. Add Tomato Sauce, olives and pepper and bring to a boil.

2. Cut each fillet into 3 or 4 pieces and carefully place in the sauce. Cover and simmer 4-5 minutes until the fish is cooked through.

3. Arrange pasta on 4 plates and top with fish and sauce. Top each serving with a teaspoonful of sour cream. Serve at once.

Makes 4 servings.

Each serving contains:

Cal	Prot	Carb	Fib	Tot. Fat	Sat. Fat	Chol	Sodium
546	33g	42g	3g	26g	4g	67mg	461mg

TUSCAN CHICKPEA SAUCE

Chickpeas, also known as *garbanzo beans*, are popular in many parts of Italy, where they turn up in pasta dishes as well as in soups and side dishes. Because they are quite chunky they go well with pasta shapes (pages 95 to 96). However this sauce from Tuscany uses a mixture of puréed and whole chickpeas to make an unusual sauce for long flat noodles. You can easily prepare this in the time it takes to cook the pasta.

1 can (14-oz. / 400g) chickpeas or garbanzo beans, drained

3 tablespoons olive oil

1 clove garlic, peeled and cut in half

2 large sprigs of fresh rosemary

4 slices smoked pancetta or lean bacon, diced

1 large onion, peeled and minced

3 tablespoons whipping cream

2 tablespoons dry white wine

Salt and pepper to taste

Cooked pasta to serve 4 people

Freshly grated Pecorino Romano cheese

1. Purée half the chickpeas or garbanzo beans in a blender or food processor and roughly chop the rest.

2. Heat oil in a large saucepan and sauté garlic and rosemary over low heat for 1-2 minutes. Remove with a slotted spoon. Add pancetta or bacon to oil and fry until crisp. Add onion and cook 3-4 minutes longer.

3. Stir in cream, wine, puréed and chopped chickpeas or garbanzos. Season to taste.

4. Toss pasta in the mixture and serve at once with grated Pecorino Romano cheese.

Makes 4 servings.

Each serving contains:

Cal	Prot	Carb	Fib	Tot. Fat	Sat. Fat	Chol	Sodium
494	16g	44g	7g	28g	8g	38mg	667mg

CARBONARA SAUCE

One story about the origin of this Roman specialty credits Umbrian charcoal burners (*carbonari*) with its invention. The ingredients are easy to carry around and the sauce could have been cooked over their open fires.

Another version suggests that the dish was invented during World War II, in response to the American allies' demands for ham and eggs.

The "ham" is usually pancetta or unsmoked bacon, but I have seen recipes which use coppa (cured shoulder of pork), prosciutto and even cooked ham. I like to serve this sauce with fettuccine but the classic choice is probably spaghetti.

1/4 lb. (115g) pancetta or unsmoked bacon, diced

1 tablespoon olive oil or melted butter

2 eggs, beaten

1 oz. (25g) freshly grated Parmesan cheese (1/4 cup)

Salt and pepper to taste

Cooked pasta to serve 4 people as a starter

1. Cook pancetta in oil or butter until crisp. In a small bowl mix eggs, cheese, salt and pepper.
2. Toss hot pasta with hot pancetta and its fat. Add egg-and-cheese mixture. Toss well until egg is cooked to desired consistency.
3. Serve at once with more Parmesan cheese and black pepper.

Makes 4 servings.

Variation

Add a little chopped onion when you cook the pancetta or use onion instead of pancetta.

Each serving contains:

Cal	Prot	Carb	Fib	Tot. Fat	Sat. Fat	Chol	Sodium
233	12g	17g	1g	13g	4g	120mg	380mg

GRASS AND HAY

The name of this modern pasta dish refers to the mixture of fresh green and yellow egg noodles, which are often served simply with butter or cream. However if you have a little time, try this version from Sienna; it will not take you more than half an hour and it makes a good dinner-party dish.

1/4 lb. (115g) unsmoked bacon, diced

1/4 lb. (115g) prosciutto, diced

2 tablespoons olive oil

1 onion, peeled and minced

1 carrot, peeled and minced

1 stalk celery, trimmed and minced

1/4 lb. (115g) brown mushrooms, minced

1 can (14-oz. / 400g) tomatoes

1/2 cup (125ml) white wine

4 oz. (115g) frozen peas

Freshly ground black pepper

Cooked pasta to serve 4 people

1. Fry bacon in a deep saucepan until crisp. Add prosciutto and then the oil.

2. Next add onion, carrot and celery and continue cooking gently for 5 minutes, stirring occasionally. Add mushrooms and cook 2 minutes longer.

3. Add tomatoes and white wine and bring to a boil. Simmer, uncovered, for 15 minutes.

4. Add peas and black pepper and simmer for another 1-2 minutes. Pour over the pasta and serve.

Makes 4 servings.

Each serving contains:

Cal	Prot	Carb	Fib	Tot. Fat	Sat. Fat	Chol	Sodium
360	16g	39g	5g	14g	3g	21mg	777mg

Chapter Four

TUBULAR PASTA

Tubular, or hollow, pasta comes in both long and short varieties. However the longer types are always broken into shorter lengths before cooking. This allows the sauce to work its way inside the smaller pieces.

Good sauces for this type of pasta usually have plenty of juice to run into the center of the tubes. Medium-size tubular pasta is often served with vegetable-based sauces but the larger penne and rigatoni will take rich meat and fish sauces.

All the types of pasta listed here are available dried; occasionally they can be found fresh. There are also whole-wheat versions of some of them.

For cooking instructions, see page xiii.

MACARONI—This is probably the best-known tubular pasta outside Italy. For the Italian market it is sold in lengths of 9 to 10 inches (23-25cm) but it is intended to be broken into smaller pieces. Outside Italy, macaroni of varying thicknesses is usually sold cut into short straight or curved pieces. The latter are known as *elbow macaroni*.

ZITI—This is really the Southern Italian name for a fairly delicate macaroni. It comes in 9-to-10-inch (23-25cm) lengths and is very popular in Sicily.

BUCATINI—This long thick pasta with hollow strands is popular in Central and Southern Italy. In the latter it is known as *perciatelli*. Like ziti, it should be broken into smaller lengths before use.

PENNE—This short tubular pasta has a smooth surface and the pieces are cut at an angle to look like quills. They are usually served with thick or rich sauces which will penetrate the hollows. *Pennete* is a shorter thinner version.

RIGATONI—These 2-to-3-inch (5-8cm) tubes are ridged along their length in order to catch some of the sauce. *Marille* is a double rigatoni created by an Italian car designer. *Ditali* are short rigatoni about 1/2 inch (1cm) long.

GARGANELLI—This is a home-made pasta from Emilia Romagna. The rolled pasta dough is cut into squares, curled around a stick and then combed to produce a ridged effect. *Trofie* is a similar pasta made in Liguria and other areas.

CAULIFLOWER AND GRILLED RED PEPPER

The idea for this sauce came from a salad served at Orso, a new-wave Italian-style restaurant in London's Covent Garden. I like the punchy combination of olives, red peppers and cauliflower even better with pasta and it looks particularly attractive with elbow macaroni.

2 large red bell peppers, seeded and quartered

1 large cauliflower, cut into florets

20 black olives, pitted

6 tablespoons whipping cream

4 sprigs fresh tarragon, chopped

Cooked pasta to serve 4 people

4 large sprigs fresh Italian parsley

1. Broil peppers until skin chars. Let stand and then peel off the skin. Cut peppers into strips.
2. Cook cauliflower 1 to 1-1/2 minutes in boiling salted water. It should still be crunchy.
3. Cut olives into quarters.
4. Place cauliflower florets, pepper strips, olives and whipping cream in a saucepan and bring to a boil. Add tarragon.
5. Spoon over pasta and garnish with sprigs of parsley.

Makes 4 servings.

Each serving contains:

Cal	Prot	Carb	Fib	Tot. Fat	Sat. Fat	Chol	Sodium
258	7g	34g	4g	12g	6g	31mg	237mg

Olives ~ *Olives are grown in almost every province of Italy. Green ones have been picked before they are fully ripe; all olives darken as they mature. Olives are hard and bitter when they are picked but table olives are cured for many months in huge vats of salt and water. The flavor of green and black olives is quite different and they are not interchangeable in recipes.*

ZUCCHINI-AND-RED-ONION SAUCE

You can vary the flavor of this simple vegetable sauce by using different herbs. I have tried fresh dill, tarragon and mint with good results. Whichever you choose, you will need to use quite a lot of it. Serve this dish following a platter of prosciutto. My favorite pasta with this sauce is ziti.

2 red onions, peeled and sliced

1/4 cup (60ml) olive oil

1/2 lb. (225g) zucchini, trimmed and cut into matchsticks

1/2 cup (125ml) fresh herbs, chopped

Salt and pepper to taste

Cooked pasta to serve 4 people

Freshly grated Parmesan cheese

1. Gently sauté onions in oil 10-12 minutes until they are very soft. Do not burn them.
2. Add zucchini and herbs. Cover and cook gently another 2-3 minutes. Season to taste.
3. Arrange pasta on 4 plates and spoon sauce over the top. Serve with freshly grated Parmesan cheese.

Makes 4 servings.

Each serving contains:

Cal	Prot	Carb	Fib	Tot. Fat	Sat. Fat	Chol	Sodium
297	8g	31g	3g	16g	3g	5mg	187mg

Red Onions ~ *These are deep purple on the outside, with a shading of pink toward the center. They fade a little as they are cooked but they do remain a pretty color. They are available year round.*

SPRING SAUCE

Now that baby vegetables are widely available in supermarkets you can recreate spring at any time of year. Keep vegetables chunky to match the pasta. Both penne and rigatoni work well.

10 baby carrots, halved lengthwise
10 baby corn, halved lengthwise
2 tablespoons peanut oil
1 tablespoon walnut or almond oil
4-5 green onions, trimmed and cut into 2-1/2-inch (6cm) lengths
8 baby zucchini, halved lengthwise
2 oz. (60g) sugar peas
2 oz. (60g) green beans, trimmed and cut into 2-1/2-inch (6cm) lengths
1 tablespoon white wine vinegar
Salt and pepper to taste
Cooked pasta to serve 4 people
Freshly grated Parmesan cheese

1. Steam carrots and corn in a small amount of water 3-4 minutes to soften.
2. Heat both oils in a wok or large skillet. Stir-fry drained carrots and corn with the green onion for 2 minutes.
3. Add remaining vegetables and continue to stir-fry until they are tender-crisp.
4. Sprinkle with vinegar, salt and pepper; toss and spoon over the pasta. Serve with freshly grated Parmesan cheese.

Makes 4 servings.

Each serving contains:

Cal	Prot	Carb	Fib	Tot. Fat	Sat. Fat	Chol	Sodium
285	9g	32g	4g	13g	3g	5mg	205mg

MANTUA SAUCE

In Mantua, winter squash is used to stuff fresh ravioli. The squash is baked, then the flesh is scraped out and mixed with Amaretti biscuits and Mostardo di Cremona, a spicy honey-and-fruit mixture. This recipe is similar but simpler. Use with short tubular pasta such as penne or macaroni. Serve with a piquant arugula or watercress salad.

1/2 lb. (225g) Hubbard or butter-nut squash, peeled and seeded

1/4 cup (60ml) sweet white wine

1/4 cup (60ml) vegetable stock

2 pkg. Amaretti biscuits, crushed

1 teaspoon English mustard

1-1/2 oz. (45g) freshly grated Parmesan cheese (6 tablespoons)

Salt and pepper to taste

Pinch of grated nutmeg

1/4 cup (60ml) half-and-half

Cooked pasta to serve 4 people as a starter

1. Place squash in a saucepan with the wine and vegetable stock. Bring to a boil. Simmer, covered, 15 minutes until squash is tender.

2. Mash with a wooden spoon and stir in remaining ingredients except pasta. Continue cooking for another minute to heat through. Toss pasta in sauce and serve at once.

Makes 4 servings.

Each serving contains:

Cal	Prot	Carb	Fib	Tot. Fat	Sat. Fat	Chol	Sodium
282	10g	40g	3g	9g	6g	14mg	347mg

Amaretti Biscuits ~ *These plump, crisp little cookies are made with a mixture of sweet and bitter almonds—it is the latter which make them taste different from other macaroons. They are usually served with coffee but they also turn up in a number of savory dishes such as this Mantua Sauce.*

ITALIAN BEAN SAUCE

Almost every Italian province has its own bean-based sauce. This version from Tuscany uses cannellini beans. In the Veneto, borlotti beans are used and celery may be omitted. Of course you may experiment with whatever beans you have on hand. Serve with penne or rigatoni and a salad of oakleaf lettuce.

1/4 cup (60ml) olive oil
1 clove garlic, peeled and minced
2 stalks celery, trimmed and minced
2 tablespoons chopped fresh parsley
2 teaspoons fresh rosemary leaves
4 firm tomatoes, seeded and diced
Salt and pepper to taste
1 can (14-oz. / 400g) cannellini or borlotti beans, drained, reserving 2 tablespoons juice
Cooked pasta to serve 4 people
Freshly grated Parmesan cheese

1. Heat olive oil in a saucepan. Add garlic, celery, parsley and rosemary and sauté gently for 2 minutes.
2. Add tomatoes, salt and pepper and toss over heat. Add beans and reserved juice. Heat through carefully and spoon over pasta. Serve with freshly grated Parmesan cheese.

Makes 4 servings.

Variations

1. For a stronger flavor stir in 1 teaspoon sun-dried-tomato paste (page 49) or 1 tablespoon tomato purée just before serving.
2. Use tarragon in place of rosemary.

Each serving contains:

Cal	Prot	Carb	Fib	Tot. Fat	Sat. Fat	Chol	Sodium
385	12g	47g	7g	17g	3g	5mg	449mg

MEXICAN CHILI SAUCE

This uncooked sauce was inspired by Mexican *salsas*, spicy relishes served with many of their main-course dishes. Green chiles give it quite a kick. The mixture can be warmed and served with hot pasta or it can be served cold as a pasta salad. It goes well with rigatoni.

Rather than chop everything by hand you can blend it in a food processor. The end result tastes just as good, although it does not look quite as interesting.

1 clove garlic, peeled and minced

4-5 green onions or 2 shallots, trimmed and minced

1 fresh green chile pepper, seeded and minced

3 firm ripe tomatoes, seeded and chopped

1 small zucchini, minced

2 tablespoons chopped fresh cilantro or coriander leaves

Salt and pepper to taste

Juice of 1 lime or 1/2 lemon

1/4 cup (60ml) olive oil

Cooked pasta to serve 4 people

Fresh cilantro or coriander sprigs

1. Place all ingredients except lime or lemon juice, oil, pasta and cilantro or coriander sprigs in a bowl.
2. Beat lime or lemon juice and oil together and pour over the vegetables. Toss together and heat, if desired.
3. Mix pasta with the sauce and serve. Garnish with fresh cilantro or coriander.

Makes 4 servings.

Variation

To make a really substantial dish add 1 can (7-oz. / 200g) drained and flaked tuna.

Each serving contains:

Cal	Prot	Carb	Fib	Tot. Fat	Sat. Fat	Chol	Sodium
270	5g	31g	3g	14g	2g	0mg	79mg

SAUCE NORMA

This eggplant-and-tomato sauce originated in Sicily long before Bellini, but it has come to be named after his opera *Norma*. Some recipes call for spaghetti but I think the chunky pieces of eggplant go well with elbow macaroni. Finish the meal with an almond tart served with the island's own dessert wine—Marsala.

1 large eggplant, sliced
Salt
1 can (14-oz. / 400g) tomatoes
1/2 clove garlic, peeled and
*   crushed*
Pinch of sugar or salt
Freshly ground black pepper
Oil for frying
3 tablespoons (20g) freshly grated
*   Parmesan cheese*
Cooked pasta to serve 4 people

Variations
1. Add 4 tablespoons chopped fresh basil before serving.
2. Add 1 teaspoon anchovy paste (page 36) to the tomatoes at the start of the sauce. Omit sugar or salt.

1. Place sliced eggplant in a colander and sprinkle with salt. Let stand 30 minutes.
2. Put tomatoes in a saucepan and add the garlic, sugar or salt, and black pepper. Bring to a boil, cover and cook 10-15 minutes to reduce. Stir occasionally.
3. Drain and pat dry eggplant slices. Pour 1 inch (2.5cm) oil into a skillet and sauté eggplant on both sides until golden.
4. Dice eggplant. Stir eggplant and freshly grated Parmesan cheese into tomato sauce.
5. Arrange pasta on 4 plates and top with the sauce. Serve with more Parmesan cheese.

Makes 4 servings.

Each serving contains:

Cal	Prot	Carb	Fib	Tot. Fat	Sat. Fat	Chol	Sodium
320	8g	38g	5g	16g	3g	4mg	330mg

MOZZARELLA-AND-TOMATO SAUCE

Mozzarella cheese gives this Tuscany sauce a thick stringy texture that goes well with short tubular pasta, particularly penne. If fresh tomatoes are not available use 2 cans (14-oz. / 400g) of tomatoes, drained. Serve with a salad of mixed greens, shredded celery and chopped parsley.

3 tablespoons olive oil

1 fresh red chile pepper, seeded and coarsely chopped

3 cloves garlic, peeled and minced

1 lb. (450g) ripe tomatoes, coarsely chopped

1/4 lb. (115g) mozzarella cheese, cut into pieces

Salt and pepper to taste

Cooked pasta to serve 4 people

1. Heat oil in a large skillet and sauté chile pepper and garlic 1-2 minutes.

2. Add tomatoes and cook 5 minutes until most of the juice from tomatoes has evaporated.

3. Add mozzarella. Lower heat and stir until cheese melts and combines with tomatoes.

4. When cheese becomes stringy, add salt, pepper and pasta. Stir with a spoon to coat each piece of pasta with sauce. Serve in deep bowls, spooning sauce over the top.

Makes 4 servings.

Each serving contains:

Cal	Prot	Carb	Fib	Tot. Fat	Sat. Fat	Chol	Sodium
321	11g	32g	2g	17g	5g	22mg	185mg

Mozzarella Cheese ~ *The best mozzarella cheese was, and still is, made with buffalo milk. Genuine mozzarella has an irregular oval shape. It is packed in whey to keep it moist. Do not buy the rectangular-shaped mozzarella, which does not come from Italy. It is often labeled "Pizza Cheese."*

ARTICHOKE MEDLEY

This recipe is a great standby if you have unexpected guests. All you have to do is raid the pantry! Chunky strips of artichoke add interesting texture to the basic tomato sauce and the chile adds a touch of heat. It goes very well with most kinds of short tubular pasta.

This quantity will serve 4 people as a starter, so double up if it is to be the main course or if you want to keep half in the refrigerator to make a cold pasta salad later in the week. It also freezes well.

1 onion, peeled and minced

1 clove garlic, peeled and minced

1 tablespoon olive oil

1 can (14-oz. / 400g) tomatoes, drained and chopped

1/4 teaspoon dried oregano

1 small dried red chile pepper, crushed, and seeded, if desired

Salt and pepper to taste

1 can (10.5-oz. / 300g) artichoke hearts, drained and cut into strips

2 tablespoons chopped fresh parsley

Cooked pasta to serve 4 people as a starter

Grated Pecorino Romano cheese

1. Gently sauté onion and garlic in the olive oil 3-4 minutes until soft. Do not allow the mixture to turn brown.
2. Add tomatoes, oregano, chile pepper, salt and pepper and bring to a boil. Cook over medium heat for 10 minutes.
3. Add artichoke hearts and parsley, heat through and spoon over the pasta. Serve with grated Pecorino Romano cheese.

Makes 4 servings.

Each serving contains:

Cal	Prot	Carb	Fib	Tot. Fat	Sat. Fat	Chol	Sodium
237	8g	29g	5g	11g	2g	7mg	689mg

GREEK SAUCE

This topping was inspired by the delicious salads served at every meal in Athens and throughout the Greek islands. The robust and fragrant flavors go well with tubular pasta. The secret is not to overcook the vegetables.

1 small onion or 6 green onions, trimmed and coarsely chopped

3 tablespoons olive oil

4 tomatoes, seeded and chopped

1 small cucumber, diced

20 black olives, pitted

2 sprigs fresh marjoram, chopped

Leaves from 2 sprigs of fresh thyme or 1/2 teaspoon dried thyme

Freshly ground black pepper

Juice of 1/2 lemon

1/4 lb. (115g) feta cheese, cubed

Cooked pasta to serve 4 people

1. Sauté onion or green onions in the oil for 1 minute. Add tomatoes, cucumber, olives, herbs and black pepper. Toss together over heat for another minute to warm through.
2. Add lemon juice and bring to a boil. Stir in cheese and cooked pasta. Toss and serve with more black pepper.

Makes 4 servings.

Variation

Instead of feta try coarsely grated Halloumi cheese. The texture will not be quite as creamy but the flavor is good.

Each serving contains:

Cal	Prot	Carb	Fib	Tot. Fat	Sat. Fat	Chol	Sodium
352	10g	36g	4g	20g	6g	25mg	526mg

PEAS AND PASTA

Fresh peas pop up in a large number of different pasta dishes but they are often variations on the same theme. Here are some ideas from various parts of Italy and from nearer home.

The first recipe comes from Puglia in the heel of Italy. It is a simple dish using fresh peas and small tubular pasta called *paternostri*. This pasta and an even smaller type called *Avemarie* are named for two of the beads on a rosary. In less-religious parts of Italy these pastas are often known as *ditalini*. The local name for the dish is *piselli e paternostri*.

In Puglia, fresh rather than frozen peas are used. After shelling, the pods are boiled in a large pan of water for 10-15 minutes. The pods are then discarded and the water is used to cook the pasta.

PEAS AND DITALINI

The dish is unusual in that the peas are dominant and the pasta is secondary. It will serve 4 people, or 6 as a starter.

2 tablespoons olive oil

1/2 clove garlic, peeled and crushed

10 sprigs Italian parsley, chopped

1 pkg. (1-lb. / 450g) frozen peas

1/4 cup (60ml) chicken or vegetable stock

Cooked pasta to serve 4 people

Salt and pepper to taste

Chopped Italian parsley

1. Heat oil in a pan and sauté garlic for 2 minutes.
2. Stir in parsley, peas and stock. Bring to a boil. Continue stirring and simmer 2-3 minutes.
3. Add pasta and toss over medium heat for a minute. Season, and serve sprinkled with chopped parsley.

Makes 4 servings.

Each serving contains:

Cal	Prot	Carb	Fib	Tot. Fat	Sat. Fat	Chol	Sodium
268	10g	40g	7g	8g	1g	0mg	243mg

PEAS WITH PANCETTA

Ham and peas are traditional partners in Italian soups and sauces, as they are elsewhere. This well-flavored recipe comes from Central Italy. It is worth seeking out pancetta for the authentic flavor it gives. If you cannot find it, unsmoked bacon can be used instead.

1 thick slice pancetta or 3 slices
  unsmoked bacon, diced
2 tablespoons olive oil
1 clove garlic, peeled and chopped
1 onion, peeled and minced
1 pkg. (10-oz. / 300g) frozen peas
1/4 cup (60ml) chicken or
  vegetable stock
Salt and pepper to taste
Cooked pasta to serve 4 people
Freshly grated Parmesan cheese

1. Sauté pancetta or bacon in oil for 1 minute. Add garlic and onion and continue cooking for 3-4 minutes until they are soft but not brown.
2. Add peas and stock and bring to a boil. Simmer 2 minutes, season with salt and pepper and toss with pasta. Serve with grated Parmesan cheese.

Makes 4 servings.

Variations
1. Add 1/2 lb. (225g) sliced fresh mushrooms and some chopped parsley with garlic and onion. Continue as above.
2. Add 1/2 lb. (225g) sliced chicken livers with garlic and onion. Sauté until cooked before adding peas.

Each serving contains:

Cal	Prot	Carb	Fib	Tot. Fat	Sat. Fat	Chol	Sodium
303	12g	36g	5g	12g	3g	9mg	388mg

PEAS WITH TOMATOES AND BASIL

A deliciously smoky aroma distinguishes this recipe from Tuscany. I came across the dish in a small restaurant in the red-brick village of Poggi Bonzi in Central Tuscany. The proprietor gave me an outline of the recipe—the rest was up to me.

2 slices smoked pancetta or 5 slices smoked bacon, diced

2 tablespoons olive oil

1 small onion, peeled and minced

1 clove garlic, peeled and crushed

1 can (14-oz. / 400g) tomatoes

Salt and pepper to taste

1 pkg. (10 oz. / 300g) frozen peas

Leaves from 3 sprigs fresh basil, roughly chopped

Cooked pasta to serve 4 people

Fresh basil sprigs

1. Sauté pancetta or bacon in oil for 2 minutes. Add onion and garlic and continue cooking 3-4 minutes until onion has softened. Do not brown.

2. Add tomatoes and juice, salt and pepper and bring to a boil. Cover and cook over medium heat 10 minutes.

3. Add peas and chopped basil and return to a boil. Cook 2-3 minutes longer. Toss with pasta and serve at once. Garnish with fresh basil.

Makes 4 servings.

Each serving contains:

Cal	Prot	Carb	Fib	Tot. Fat	Sat. Fat	Chol	Sodium
307	11g	40g	6g	12g	2g	7mg	436mg

SUMMER SAUCE

I call this *Summer Sauce* because it is best made with fresh garden peas and tomatoes. However it can also be made with frozen peas. In this case boil the cream sauce for an additional 1-2 minutes before adding the peas.

The sauce goes well with any kind of tubular pasta. Serve with a salad of oakleaf lettuce and crusty whole-wheat rolls.

2 tablespoons melted butter
2 tablespoons olive oil
8-10 green onions, chopped
1/2 lb. (225g) small button
  mushrooms, halved
1 cup (250ml) whipping cream
1/2 (125ml) cup vegetable stock
Salt and pepper to taste
1/2 lb. (225g) fresh or frozen peas
4 small tomatoes, chopped
Cooked pasta to serve 4 people
Freshly grated Parmesan cheese

1. Heat butter and oil in a saucepan and sauté green onions until soft. Add mushrooms and cook 2-3 minutes.

2. Add cream, stock, salt and pepper and bring to a boil. Boil rapidly 2-3 minutes.

3. Add peas and cook until peas are tender and sauce has thickened. Add tomatoes. Return to a boil and cook 1 minute before serving. Spoon over pasta and serve with freshly grated Parmesan cheese.

Makes 4 servings.

Variations

1. Use yogurt instead of cream. Stabilize with 1 tablespoon cornstarch, potato starch or flour.

2. Serve sprinkled with 2 tablespoons chopped fresh chervil.

Each serving contains:

Cal	Prot	Carb	Fib	Tot. Fat	Sat. Fat	Chol	Sodium
556	13g	44g.	7g	37g	20g	102mg	346mg

SHRIMP-AND-GREEN-OLIVE SAUCE

Shrimp abound in the fish markets of Provence and they are used in all kinds of dishes. The idea for this sauce came from a restaurant in Toulon where jumbo shrimp were served with large pasta shells in a creamy sauce. I find the recipe works well with ordinary peeled shrimp and tubular pasta. Serve with a salad of young spinach leaves dressed in a light extra-virgin olive oil.

2 tablespoons (25g) butter

2 cloves garlic, peeled and crushed

Grated peel of 1 lemon

4 tomatoes, seeded and chopped

12 green olives, pitted and quartered

1/2 cup (125ml) whipping cream

3 tablespoons dry white wine

1/2 lb. (225g) cooked shrimp

Salt and pepper to taste

3 tablespoons chopped fresh basil or tarragon

Cooked pasta to serve 4 people

1. Melt butter in a pan and sauté garlic and lemon peel for 1 minute. Add tomatoes and olives and toss well.

2. Pour in cream and wine and bring to a boil. Simmer for 5 minutes.

3. Toss in shrimp, salt, pepper and fresh basil or tarragon and heat through.

4. Pour sauce over pasta and serve with more black pepper.

Makes 4 servings.

Each serving contains:

Cal	Prot	Carb	Fib	Tot. Fat	Sat. Fat	Chol	Sodium
380	18g	32g	3g	20g	11g	167mg	557mg

PROSCIUTTO-AND-MUSHROOM SAUCE

Whenever I see air-dried hams hanging in the delicatessen I am reminded of the rows of hams I saw hanging in the sheds of Parma. Prosciutto and porcini mushrooms give an authentic Italian flavor to this sauce from that area. You can substitute cultivated mushrooms and smoked ham for a milder flavor.

Serve with a mixed-green salad lightly dressed with extra-virgin olive oil and a good red wine vinegar. Garnish with shredded green peppers.

2 oz. (60g) dried porcini mushrooms

1/4 lb. (115g) prosciutto

1/4 lb. (115g) boiled ham

1 red onion, peeled and minced

1 tablespoon butter

2 tablespoons olive oil

1 can (14-oz. / 400g) chopped tomatoes

1/2 cup (125ml) whipping cream

Salt and pepper to taste

Cooked pasta to serve 4 people

Freshly grated Parmesan cheese

1. Cover dried mushrooms with boiling water and let stand 15-20 minutes. Drain, reserving liquid for another dish.
2. Finely chop together prosciutto, ham and soaked mushrooms.
3. Sauté onion in butter and oil 2-3 minutes. Do not brown.
4. Add meat mixture and chopped tomatoes and stir well.
5. Bring to a boil and cook, partially covered, 10-15 minutes to thicken sauce.
6. Stir in cream, heat and season with salt and pepper. Spoon over pasta and serve with grated Parmesan cheese.

Makes 4 servings.

Each serving contains:

Cal	Prot	Carb	Fib	Tot. Fat	Sat. Fat	Chol	Sodium
510	27g	40g	5g	27g	12g	64mg	1145mg

PROSCIUTTO-AND-GOAT-CHEESE SAUCE

Some traditional restaurants in Italy serve a set meal of dishes chosen daily by the chef as he shops in the local market. This sauce, served with thick penne, formed part of a gargantuan seven-course meal in just such a restaurant in the old part of Pescara on the Adriatic coast. Goat cheese was the strongest flavor, so vegetarians could leave out the prosciutto and still have a tasty sauce. It makes an excellent supper dish served with a tomato-and-basil salad.

1 onion, peeled and minced

2 tablespoons cooking oil

2 tablespoons dry white wine

2 tablespoons vegetable or chicken stock

6 oz. (175g) fresh well-flavored goat cheese, cubed

1/4 cup (50g) prosciutto, diced

Freshly ground black pepper

Cooked pasta to serve 4 people

Freshly grated hard goat cheese or Pecorino Romano cheese

1. Sauté onion in oil 2-3 minutes until soft but not brown.
2. Add wine and stock and stir in the cheese. When the cheese has melted completely, stir in prosciutto and black pepper and heat through.
3. Toss cooked pasta in sauce and serve with freshly ground black pepper and grated goat or Pecorino Romano cheese.

Makes 4 servings.

Each serving contains:

Cal	Prot	Carb	Fib	Tot. Fat	Sat. Fat	Chol	Sodium
427	22g	28g	2g	24g	13g	56mg	364mg

Prosciutto ~ *This is the general name given to any kind of air-dried ham. The best-known variety is probably Parma ham. You can also buy San Danielle and prosciutto crudo. The latter is usually less costly as it does not come from a specific area.*

ITALIAN-SAUSAGE-AND-PEPPER SAUCE

Italian sausages are 100 percent meat and have their own distinctive and aromatic flavor. They make a fairly heavy sauce that is good with tubular pasta such as rigatoni or ziti.

6 small Italian sausages
(about 8 oz. / 225g in total)

1 onion, peeled and minced

1 tablespoon olive oil

1 large red bell pepper, seeded and cut into short strips

2 large ripe tomatoes, skinned, seeded and coarsely chopped

1/2 cup (125ml) red wine

1/4 cup (60ml) vegetable stock or water

Pinch of fennel seed

Pinch of dried oregano

Pinch of dried thyme

Salt and pepper to taste

Cooked pasta to serve 4 people as a starter

1. Prick sausages all over with a fork and place in a pan with 1/4 inch (5mm) water. Bring to a boil and simmer 20 minutes. When water evaporates, sausages will fry in their own fat. Cook 10 minutes longer, turning occasionally. Drain on a paper towel.

2. In another pan sauté the onion in olive oil 5-6 minutes until lightly browned. Add red bell pepper and cook 2-3 minutes longer. Add remaining ingredients except pasta. Bring to a boil, reduce heat and simmer 20 minutes. Add more stock if necessary.

3. Slice sausages and mix with sauce. Serve on hot pasta.

Makes 4 servings.

Each serving contains:

Cal	Prot	Carb	Fib	Tot. Fat	Sat. Fat	Chol	Sodium
351	15g	26g	3g	19g	6g	44mg	602mg

PORK-AND-BRANDY SAUCE

This rich meat sauce comes from Leghorn on the Tuscan coast. There it is served with penne or rigatoni. If you prefer you could also serve it with spiral-shaped fusilli. Despite its meat base it does not take very long to cook. I usually chop the meat in a food processor but you need to be careful not to over-process it. Serve with a crunchy salad of apples, celery and walnuts.

1 onion, peeled and minced

2 cloves garlic, peeled and crushed

2 tablespoons olive oil

6 oz. (175g) ham, minced

6 oz. (175g) lean pork, minced

1 small bunch of fresh basil, roughly chopped

1/4 teaspoon dried thyme

1/4 teaspoon paprika

1/4 cup (60ml) brandy

Salt and pepper to taste

Cooked pasta to serve 4 people

Freshly grated Parmesan cheese

1. Sauté onion and garlic in oil for 3-4 minutes until soft.
2. Add ham and pork and brown all over.
3. Add remaining ingredients except pasta and cheese and bring to a boil. Cover and simmer for 10 minutes.
4. Mix pasta into sauce and toss together. Serve with freshly grated Parmesan cheese.

Makes 4 servings.

Variation

Add 2-3 tablespoons frozen peas with the brandy and other flavorings.

Each serving contains:

Cal	Prot	Carb	Fib	Tot. Fat	Sat. Fat	Chol	Sodium
401	31g	27g	2g	14g	4g	68mg	777mg

Chapter Five

PASTA SHAPES

Many different and intriguing pasta shapes are available. Some are traditional; other shapes have been dreamed up by dried-pasta manufacturers both here and in Italy. I like to use sauces with plenty of juice to fill pockets and interesting textures to match the pasta shapes. The simple sauces in Chapter 1 work well too.

All the pasta types listed below are available dried but they can rarely be bought fresh outside Italy. There are also whole-wheat and flavored versions of many of them.

For cooking instructions, see page xiii.

CAVATIEDDI is a small mussel-shaped pasta from Apulia, usually handmade.

CONCHIGLIE is shell-shaped. Smaller shells are known as *conchigliette.*

CORZETTI is a figure-eight shape from Liguria.

FARFALLE is butterfly- or bow-shaped. It looks good with chunky sauces.

FUSILLI, a spiral-shaped pasta, comes in a variety of thicknesses.

ORECCHIETTE, or *little ears*, comes from Apulia. It takes longer to cook than some other shapes.

ROTELLE is a wheel-shaped pasta not widely found in Italy.

CAULIFLOWER-AND-SAFFRON SAUCE

The rich, vibrant color of this Sicilian sauce comes from the saffron. Because this distinctively flavored spice is so expensive this sauce is usually served only on holidays. I like to serve it with orecchiette, which is not a local choice, or fusilli, which is. In Sicily the water-conscious locals use the water the cauliflower has been cooked in to cook the pasta.

1 medium-sized cauliflower

1/4 cup (60ml) olive oil

2 cloves garlic, peeled and crushed

1/4 teaspoon saffron strands or powder

3 tomatoes, seeded and chopped

1 tablespoon raisins or sultanas

1 tablespoon pine nuts, toasted (page xiv)

Salt and pepper to taste

Cooked pasta to serve 4 people

Freshly grated Pecorino Sardo cheese

1. Cover cauliflower with boiling water and cook 6-8 minutes. Drain, reserving water to cook pasta. Cut cauliflower into florets. (I set the stalks aside to use in soup but you can add them to the sauce.)

2. Heat oil in a pan and sauté garlic and saffron 1 minute. Add cauliflower florets and stir-fry until cauliflower is crisp-tender.

3. Add tomatoes, raisins or sultanas, pine nuts, salt, pepper and 3 tablespoons cauliflower water. Stir-fry another 1-2 minutes to heat through.

4. Toss pasta with sauce. Serve with Pecorino Sardo cheese.

Makes 4 servings.

Each serving contains:

Cal	Prot	Carb	Fib	Tot. Fat	Sat. Fat	Chol	Sodium
352	11g	36g	4g	20g	4g	5mg	215mg

BLUE-CHEESE-AND-BROCCOLI SAUCE

Broccoli and blue cheese blend well with pasta. Choose a mild and creamy cheese. Heat brings out the flavor, so a cheese like Gorgonzola would probably be too overpowering. For a particularly attractive dish use green and red spirals mixed with plain fusilli.

The faster you cook the broccoli, the better the texture and the quicker you will get your meal! Serve with a grated-carrot-and-celery salad.

1/2 lb. (225g) broccoli or calabrese
1 tablespoon olive oil
1 small onion, peeled and minced
1/2 cup (125ml) dry white wine
1/4 cup (60ml) whipping cream
1/4 lb. (115g) mild blue cheese
  such as Blue Brie, Cambozola
  or Dolcelatte, cubed
Freshly ground black pepper
Cooked pasta to serve 4 people
Fresh parsley sprigs

1. Cook broccoli or calabrese in lightly salted, boiling water for 6-7 minutes until tender-crisp. Drain and cut into florets. Cut the stems into pieces.

2. Heat oil in a pan and sauté onion 2-3 minutes until soft. Add white wine and cream and bring to a boil. Add cubed cheese and pepper and stir until cheese is melted.

3. Toss broccoli or calabrese with pasta and pour sauce on top. Garnish with sprigs of parsley and serve at once.

Makes 4 servings.

Each serving contains:

Cal	Prot	Carb	Fib	Tot. Fat	Sat. Fat	Chol	Sodium
343	12g	30g	3g	18g	9g	42mg	419mg

CHICKPEAS WITH OIL & FLAVORINGS

One of the simplest pasta sauces I have come across is a traditional dish from Basilica in Southern Italy. The chickpeas, or garbanzos, are dressed with clove-flavored onions and served with farfalle. Recipes from other areas use tomato sauce, prosciutto and arugula.

CHICKPEAS WITH ONIONS AND CLOVES

This is a slightly more-elaborate version of the Basilican dish. Use canned chickpeas or garbanzos for speed but discard the liquid from the can.

1/4 cup (60ml) extra-virgin olive oil

3 cloves

2 large onions, peeled and sliced

1 can (7-oz. / 200g) chickpeas or garbanzos, drained

3 tablespoons well-flavored vegetable or chicken stock

Salt and pepper to taste

1 teaspoon tomato purée (optional)

Cooked pasta to serve 4 people

Freshly grated Parmesan cheese

1. Heat oil in a large pan and sauté cloves for 1 minute. Add onions and cook until lightly browned. Remove cloves.

2. Stir in chickpeas or garbanzos and stock and cook another minute. Season to taste, adding tomato purée if desired.

3. Toss with pasta and serve with grated Parmesan cheese.

Makes 4 servings.

Each serving contains:

Cal	Prot	Carb	Fib	Tot. Fat	Sat. Fat	Chol	Sodium
344	10g	38g	5g	17g	3g	5mg	329mg

CHICKPEAS WITH PROSCIUTTO AND ARUGULA

The bitter flavor of the arugula, or rocket, complements that of the chickpeas in this classic from the city of Potenza in the Southern Appenines. When I ate there, gnarled olive trees clung to the hillsides below the restaurant terrace and the air was full of the scent of the proprietor's herb garden.

1/4 cup (60ml) extra-virgin olive oil

3 tablespoons chopped fresh parsley

1 tablespoon chopped fresh tarragon

1/2 teaspoon grated lemon peel

1/2 cup (125ml) coarsely chopped arugula

2 oz. (50g) prosciutto, diced

1 can (7-oz. / 200g) chickpeas or garbanzos, drained

Cooked pasta to serve 4 people

Freshly ground black pepper

Freshly grated Parmesan cheese

1. Heat oil in a large saucepan and sauté fresh herbs, arugula and lemon peel for 1 minute. Add prosciutto and chickpeas or garbanzos and mix well.

2. Add pasta and black pepper and toss together. Serve with grated Parmesan cheese.

Makes 4 servings.

Each serving contains:

Cal	Prot	Carb	Fib	Tot. Fat	Sat. Fat	Chol	Sodium
340	12g	33g	4g	18g	3g	12mg	434mg

TURKISH TAHINI SAUCE

This Turkish sauce is usually served on baked fish or steamed vegetables such as beans or cauliflower. I have adapted it to serve with pasta shapes. A green salad completes the meal.

1/4 lb. (115g) shelled walnuts

1 clove garlic

1/2 teaspoon salt

4 tablespoons tahini paste

2 tablespoons lemon juice

1/4 cup (60ml) chopped fresh parsley

5-6 tablespoons water

Cooked pasta to serve 4 people

1. Place all ingredients except pasta in a blender or food processor and blend until desired consistency. Do not overblend or you will lose the rough texture provided by the walnuts.
2. Transfer to a saucepan and heat gently, adding more water as the mixture thickens. Do not allow sauce to boil.
3. Toss pasta in sauce and serve at once.

Makes 4 servings.

Each serving contains:

Cal	Prot	Carb	Fib	Tot. Fat	Sat. Fat	Chol	Sodium
397	11g	33g	4g	27g	3g	0mg	273mg

Tahini Paste ~ *This paste, consisting of ground sesame seeds, is used throughout the Middle East. It can be made at home but it is quicker and easier to use a jar of ready-made tahini paste, available from delicatessens and some supermarkets.*

ZUCCHINI-AND-GARLIC SAUCE

There are lots of zucchini recipes but I think this one is the best. The flavors of the onion, garlic and zucchini blend beautifully and the basil sets it all off well. Serve with any kind of pasta shape.

2 onions, peeled and sliced
2 cloves garlic, peeled and crushed
1/4 cup (50g) butter
1 tablespoon olive oil
3/4 lb. (340g) zucchini, cubed
Salt and pepper to taste
10 basil leaves, torn into pieces
Cooked pasta to serve 4 people
Butter
Freshly grated Parmesan cheese

1. Gently sauté onion and garlic in butter and oil. Do not allow them to burn.
2. After 3-4 minutes add zucchini, salt and pepper and continue cooking gently until zucchini are tender. This will take 15-20 minutes, depending on the size of the cubes.
3. Add basil leaves and pasta. Toss and serve topped with a pat of butter and freshly grated Parmesan cheese.

Makes 4 servings.

Each serving contains:

Cal	Prot	Carb	Fib	Tot. Fat	Sat. Fat	Chol	Sodium
315	9g	32g	3g	18g	9g	36mg	306mg

SICILIAN EGGPLANT SAUCE

Eggplant is a great favorite in Sicily so no market is complete without great mounds of this beautifully shiny, deep-purple vegetable. It crops up in many sauces with a lot of different ingredients and flavorings. Here toasted nuts and seeds give a slightly crunchy texture.

I think this particular sauce goes well with rotelle, the pasta shaped like small wheels. Serve with a mixed-leaf salad, including arugula or watercress, dressed with yogurt and lemon juice.

1 tablespoon pine nuts

1 tablespoon sunflower seeds

2 cloves garlic, peeled and crushed

5 tablespoons olive oil

1-1/2 tablespoons sun-dried-tomato paste (page 49)

1 large eggplant, diced

4 tomatoes, coarsely chopped

4 tablespoons chopped fresh parsley

Salt and pepper to taste

Cooked pasta to serve 4 people

8-12 black olives

Fresh parsley sprigs

1. Toast pine nuts and sunflower seeds in a dry skillet.

2. Sauté garlic in oil and add sun-dried tomato paste. Stir and add eggplant. Cook gently over low heat 8-12 minutes until tender (do not allow it to become mushy).

3. Add tomatoes, chopped parsley, toasted nuts and seeds, salt and pepper and cook for another 2-3 minutes.

4. Spoon over pasta and garnish with black olives and sprigs of fresh parsley.

Makes 4 servings.

Each serving contains:

Cal	Prot	Carb	Fib	Tot. Fat	Sat. Fat	Chol	Sodium
377	8g	40g	6g	23g	3g	0mg	226mg

CAULIFLOWER SAUCE

This is one of many vegetable sauces served as a starter with Puglia's famous "little ears" pasta, or orecchiette. This pasta is not often made at home now but I have seen women making it by hand in the back streets of Bari and Brindisi on the Adriatic.

1 small cauliflower or 1/2 large one

Salt

2 whole cloves garlic, peeled

5 anchovy fillets in oil, drained, or 2 teaspoons anchovy paste (page 36)

3 tablespoons olive oil

Cooked pasta to serve 4 people as a starter

Freshly ground black pepper

Leaves from 10 large parsley sprigs

1/2 teaspoon hot-red-pepper flakes or chili oil (page 108)

Variation

Use broccoli in place of cauliflower. Top with toasted pine nuts rather than parsley.

1. Cut cauliflower into florets and discard stalks. Cover florets and garlic with boiling salted water and boil for 1 minute. Drain cooking liquid into another pan and use it to cook the pasta. Discard garlic and keep cauliflower warm.

2. Sauté anchovy fillets in olive oil and mash into a paste. Toss cooked pasta in this paste. (Or use commercial anchovy paste and omit olive oil.) Add cauliflower, season to taste and toss over low heat.

3. Sprinkle with parsley leaves and red-pepper flakes or chili oil and serve at once.

Makes 4 servings.

Each serving contains:

Cal	Prot	Carb	Fib	Tot. Fat	Sat. Fat	Chol	Sodium
196	5g	19g	2g	11g	2g	4mg	267mg

RICH RICOTTA SAUCE

The classic version of this sauce, which was first cooked for me by a friend who lives in Rome, is made with a mild ewe's-milk ricotta. However I have made it with the more strongly flavored goat's-milk ricotta and with fresh goat cheese. Other cheeses which work well include garlic and herb roulades and Boursin.

This sauce is quite thick but still manages to get into the hollows and folds of most pasta shapes. Serve with a raw spinach salad.

1/2 recipe Neapolitan Tomato Sauce (page 26)

1 cup (250ml) whipping cream

4 oz. (115g) ricotta or fresh goat cheese, slightly mashed

Freshly ground black pepper

Cooked pasta to serve 4 people

Freshly grated Parmesan cheese

1. Heat Tomato Sauce in a pan and stir in cream. Bring mixture to a simmer.
2. Add cheese and black pepper and heat through. Pour over pasta and toss well together.
3. Serve with freshly grated Parmesan cheese.

Makes 4 servings.

Variation
Add chopped fresh herbs just before serving.

Each serving contains:

Cal	Prot	Carb	Fib	Tot. Fat	Sat. Fat	Chol	Sodium
562	15g	44g	2g	37g	18g	103mg	265mg

ARUGULA SAUCE

The Italians like the pungent flavor of rocket, or arugula. In addition to putting it in salads, they use it to great effect with pasta. It makes an interesting sauce base when mixed with a sharp, full-flavored cheese like Pecorino Romano. There's not much cooking involved either!

I often serve this dish as a main course, starting with a plate of prosciutto and melon and finishing with tiramisu for dessert.

5 tablespoons extra-virgin olive oil
2 cloves garlic, peeled and crushed
1-2 small whole dried red chiles
Cooked pasta to serve 4 people
1/2 small bunch (50g) arugula or Swiss chard, roughly torn
Freshly grated Pecorino Romano cheese

1. Heat olive oil in a large skillet and sauté garlic and chiles 1-2 minutes until brown. Discard chiles.
2. Add pasta and arugula or Swiss chard to the pan. Toss well together and serve with freshly grated Pecorino Romano cheese.

Makes 4 servings.

Each serving contains:

Cal	Prot	Carb	Fib	Tot. Fat	Sat. Fat	Chol	Sodium
305	7g	27g	1g	19g	3g	7mg	81mg

Pecorino Cheese *~ Pecorino cheese is the general name for ewe's-milk cheese made in Central and Southern Italy. Each area produces cheese with its own characteristics. Pecorino Romano is aged for eight months. It is hard, salty and piquant and is best used for grating. Pecorino Tuscano is almost always eaten when it is young and soft. Pecorino Sardo can be eaten when it is still quite young and fresh but it will harden and gain in piquancy as it ages. Young Pecorino is known as "Pecorino Fresco."*

ARUGULA-AND-TOMATO SAUCE

If you are not sure you like the flavor of arugula, or rocket, try boiling it with the pasta. It is not as pungent cooked this way and the tomato sauce will supply the flavor. Arugula looks very attractive with pasta bows or shells. Make sure you have plenty of freshly grated grana cheese, which is similar to Parmesan.

1 small bunch (115g) arugula
Pinch of salt
1 teaspoon olive oil
8-12 oz. (225-340g) uncooked dried pasta
1 recipe Classic Tomato Sauce (page 25)
Freshly grated grana cheese

Variation
Use Swiss chard instead of arugula.

1. Place arugula in a large pan filled with water. Bring to a boil and add salt, olive oil and pasta. Cook as directed on the pasta package.
2. Make Tomato Sauce or reheat from the refrigerator or freezer.
3. Drain pasta and arugula and spoon onto 4 plates. Top with Tomato Sauce and serve with freshly grated grana cheese.

Makes 4 servings.

Each serving contains:

Cal	Prot	Carb	Fib	Tot. Fat	Sat. Fat	Chol	Sodium
450	16g	59g	4g	17g	4g	10mg	631mg

BEAN-AND-ONION SAUCE

This recipe comes from Puglia where it is served with home-made orecchiette or cavatieddi.

1 can (14-oz. / 400g) cannellini or haricot beans, drained

1/4 cup (60ml) olive oil

2 cloves garlic, peeled and halved

3 whole dried red chile peppers

2 bay leaves

2 red onions, peeled and sliced

3 stalks celery, trimmed and sliced, or 1/2 teaspoon celery salt

2 tablespoons white or red wine

3-4 tablespoons vegetable stock or water

Salt and pepper to taste

Cooked pasta to serve 4 people

Chili oil

1. Purée beans in a food processor or rub through a sieve.
2. Heat oil in a pan and sauté garlic, chiles and bay leaves until well browned. Remove from the oil with a slotted spoon and discard.
3. Sauté onions and celery or celery salt in the flavored oil 4-5 minutes until golden. Add bean purée, wine, stock or water, salt and pepper and bring to a boil.
4. Spoon over pasta and serve with a little chili oil.

Makes 4 servings.

Each serving contains:

Cal	Prot	Carb	Fib	Tot. Fat	Sat. Fat	Chol	Sodium
418	9g	47g	7g	21g	3g	0mg	295mg

Chili oil ~ *Spicy flavors are popular in Southern Italy and most cooks will have a special chili oil on hand. This can be bought or made at home by steeping 2-3 dried red chile peppers in a jar of olive oil for 2-3 weeks.*

ITALIAN CRUNCHY SAUCE

I first tried this mixture as a stuffing for grilled vegetables and liked it so much that I looked for other ways to use the same flavor combination. Pasta was the answer. The distinctively flavored ingredients make a wonderful sauce with an interesting crunchy texture. I often serve it as a starter with spirals but you could use bows or wheels.

2 tablespoons sultanas or raisins

2 tablespoons capers

2 tablespoons toasted pine nuts

24 black olives, pitted and quartered

1/2 clove garlic, peeled and crushed

6 green onions, trimmed and chopped

Freshly ground black pepper

6-8 tablespoons extra-virgin olive oil

Cooked pasta to serve 4 people as a starter

2 tablespoons chopped fresh parsley

Variation

Add 3-4 chopped anchovy fillets to the mixture.

1. Cover sultanas or raisins and capers with water. Let stand 10-15 minutes, changing water once, until softened.

2. Drain caper mixture and chop with the pine nuts and olives or chop in a food processor.

3. Mix in garlic, green onions, black pepper and 4-6 tablespoons oil (reserving 2 tablespoons). Spoon into a small shallow heatproof dish, place under the broiler and cook 3-4 minutes, stirring occasionally.

4. Toss pasta in remaining oil and add vegetable mixture. Toss again and serve sprinkled with chopped parsley and more black pepper.

Makes 4 servings.

Each serving contains:

Cal	Prot	Carb	Fib	Tot. Fat	Sat. Fat	Chol	Sodium
406	5g	24g	3g	34g	5g	0mg	397mg

COLD SEAFOOD-AND-BASIL SAUCE

This shell-pasta dish served on a bed of lettuce is perfect on summer evenings. It can be eaten warm or at room temperature. The original recipe specifies shrimps, scallops and squid but any mixture of ready-prepared shellfish can be used.

1/2 lb. (225g) mixed cooked shell-fish, seasoned with a little salt

Cooked pasta to serve 4 people

1 small red bell pepper, seeded and diced

4-5 green onions, trimmed and chopped

1/3 cup (75g) cooked petit peas

3 tablespoons chopped fresh basil

2 tablespoons chopped fresh parsley

Pinch of dried thyme or oregano

6 tablespoons olive oil

1 tablespoon lemon juice

Salt and pepper to taste

1 tablespoon capers, drained

1. Toss shellfish and pasta with red peppers, green onions and peas. If you prefer to serve the dish warm, do this as soon as the pasta is cooked and drained.

2. Beat together herbs, olive oil, lemon juice, salt and pepper. Heat gently in a pan if serving warm, but do not allow mixture to boil. Pour over pasta mixture.

3. Spoon onto 4 plates and sprinkle with capers and more black pepper. Serve at once.

Makes 4 servings.

Each serving contains:

Cal	Prot	Carb	Fib	Tot. Fat	Sat. Fat	Chol	Sodium
375	17g	28g	2g	22g	3g	111mg	197mg

SALMON-AND-WALNUT SAUCE

Even though salmon is not a native of the Mediterranean it often appears on Italian menus. This sauce comes from a restaurant perched on a rocky promontory just outside San Remo on the Italian Riviera. We sat in the sunshine looking out over the sea and downing a glass of the local wine. The sauce was served with corzetti, a local pasta shape. It is also good with fusilli.

3/4 lb. (340g) fresh salmon steak
3 tablespoons olive oil
1 onion, peeled and sliced
1/3 cup (80ml) white wine
3 tablespoons tomato purée
Salt and pepper to taste
1 tablespoon chopped fresh basil
  or parsley
8 walnut halves, minced
Cooked pasta to serve 4 people

Variation
  You can use canned salmon or tuna in place of fresh fish. Canned tuna works better than canned salmon, although the flavor is different.

1. Skin and fillet salmon. Boil bones with a little water to make fish stock. Cut the fish into thin strips.
2. Heat oil in a pan and sauté onion for 2-3 minutes until soft but not brown. Add salmon and cook 5 minutes more, stirring constantly.
3. Add wine, 1/3 cup (75ml) fish stock, tomato purée, salt and pepper and bring to a boil. Simmer 5 minutes.
4. Add half the basil or parsley and half the walnuts. Blend in a food processor until smooth.
5. Reheat and stir in pasta and remaining basil or parsley and walnuts. Toss well together and serve with more black pepper.

Makes 4 servings.

Each serving contains:

Cal	Prot	Carb	Fib	Tot. Fat	Sat. Fat	Chol	Sodium
407	23g	29g	2g	21g	3g	53mg	156mg

MONKFISH-AND-TOMATO SAUCE

Choose a large size of conchiglie for this dish so the sauce can gather in delicious pools inside the pasta shells. Cut monkfish into pieces of about the same size so that the dish is chunky in appearance.

2 cloves garlic, peeled and chopped

1 onion, peeled and minced

2 tablespoons olive oil

1 can (24-oz. / 750ml) tomato juice

2 teaspoons tomato purée

1/2 cup (125ml) dry white wine or fish stock

Salt and pepper to taste

8 small monkfish fillets

Cooked pasta to serve 4 people

4-6 sprigs of fresh basil

1. Gently sauté garlic and onion in oil until soft but not brown.

2. Add tomato juice, tomato purée, wine or stock, salt and pepper. Bring to a boil, reduce heat and simmer 8-10 minutes until sauce has thickened as desired.

3. Cube monkfish fillets and add to sauce. Cook 4-6 minutes longer, until fish is cooked. Be careful not to overcook or the fish will become hard.

4. Pour over pasta and toss together gently.

5. Garnish with sprigs of basil and serve at once.

Makes 4 servings.

Each serving contains:

Cal	Prot	Carb	Fib	Tot. Fat	Sat. Fat	Chol	Sodium
350	27g	34g	2g	10g	1g	36mg	720mg

FLORENTINE SAUCE WITH GREEN PEPPERCORNS

Dishes cooked with spinach are often described as *Florentine* because the citizens of Florence have always had a preference for this vegetable. However this colorful pasta sauce comes from my Roman friend's repertoire and she is not sure where it originated! It is vital to add the spinach at the last minute, or it will become limp.

The sauce looks very pretty with bows, butterflies or wheels.

1/4 lb. (115g) salami

1/4 lb. (115g) smoked ham

Cooked pasta to serve 4 people

2 tablespoons olive oil

1/4 lb. (115g) spinach or Swiss chard leaves, shredded

2 tablespoons green peppercorns

Freshly ground black pepper

Freshly grated Parmesan cheese

1. Skin and dice salami and cut ham into small thin strips.
2. Add to pasta and toss over a low heat to warm thoroughly.
3. Add oil, spinach or Swiss chard, green peppercorns and black pepper and serve with freshly grated Parmesan cheese.

Makes 4 servings.

Each serving contains:

Cal	Prot	Carb	Fib	Tot. Fat	Sat. Fat	Chol	Sodium
316	16g	26g	2g	16g	5g	37mg	810mg

Swiss Chard ~ *This green vegetable has large flat leaves which taste very much like spinach. The stalks are much thicker and more pronounced and can be sliced and cooked as a vegetable in their own right. If they are to be served with the leaves they will need a slightly longer cooking time.*

113

WILD-MUSHROOM-AND-PANCETTA SAUCE

The flavor of this sauce is punchy and robust. I usually serve it with fusilli. It doesn't take a great deal to flavor a bowlful so don't worry if you think there isn't enough! Serve with sliced cucumber marinated in a light vinegar dressing.

1-1/2 to 2 oz. (35-50g) dried mixed wild mushrooms

2 tablespoons tomato purée

2 teaspoons sun-dried-tomato paste (page 49)

2 thick slices pancetta or unsmoked bacon (about 6 oz. / 175g)

1 onion, peeled and minced

2 cloves garlic, peeled and crushed

Salt and pepper to taste

Cooked pasta to serve 4 people

1. Place mushrooms in a bowl and cover with boiling water. Let stand 20 minutes.

2. Drain, reserving liquid, and chop. Mix liquid with tomato purée and paste.

3. Sauté rind and fat from the pancetta in a small pan. Cube remaining meat.

4. Remove bits of rind from the pan and sauté onion and garlic until golden. Add lean diced pancetta and cook a minute longer. Add chopped mushrooms, tomato-paste mixture, salt and pepper.

5. Bring to a boil and cook about 5 minutes until sauce is fairly thick. Stir occasionally.

6. Spoon over pasta, toss and serve at once.

Makes 4 servings.

Each serving contains:

Cal	Prot	Carb	Fib	Tot. Fat	Sat. Fat	Chol	Sodium
422	19g	38g	3g	22g	8g	36mg	792mg

HARLEQUIN PASTA

The colorful mixture of red peppers, sweet corn and peas inspired the name of this dish. It's colorful and attractive and fun to serve when you are entertaining friends. Butterfly or bow shapes are the prettiest choice. For the best results, keep the meatballs small so they do not dwarf the pasta shapes.

3/4 lb. (340g) ground lamb

1 teaspoon chopped fresh mint

1 tablespoon chopped fresh parsley

Pinch of chili powder or cayenne pepper

Salt and pepper to taste

2 tablespoons olive oil

1 clove garlic, peeled and crushed

1 can (14oz. / 400g) chopped tomatoes, drained

1 red bell pepper, seeded and diced

1/4 cup (50g) frozen peas

1/4 cup (50g) frozen corn

Cooked pasta to serve 4 people

Fresh mint sprigs

1. Mix ground lamb with mint, parsley, chili powder or cayenne, salt and pepper. Shape into tiny balls.

2. Heat 1 tablespoon olive oil in a skillet over high heat. Add meatballs and sauté until browned. Reduce the heat and cook another 2-3 minutes.

3. In a saucepan, mix garlic, tomatoes and remaining olive oil and simmer 5 minutes.

4. Add red bell pepper, peas and corn and continue cooking 5 minutes until vegetables are tender.

5. Toss all ingredients with pasta and serve garnished with sprigs of mint.

Makes 4 servings.

Each serving contains:

Cal	Prot	Carb	Fib	Tot. Fat	Sat. Fat	Chol	Sodium
442	28g	33g	3g	22g	7g	79mg	296mg

CHICKEN-LIVER SAUCE

This tasty, rich sauce goes particularly well with orecchiette. It makes a good special-occasion first course. Follow with veal or pork medallions in lemon-and-butter sauce, green beans and a salad.

2 tablespoons (25g) butter

1/2 onion, peeled and minced

3 tablespoons chopped fresh parsley

1/2 lb. (225g) chicken livers, chopped

1 teaspoon flour

2 tablespoons Vin Santo or sweet white wine

Salt and pepper to taste

1/2 cup (125ml) whipping cream

Cooked pasta to serve 4 people as a starter

Freshly grated Parmesan cheese

1. Melt butter in a pan and add onion, parsley and chicken livers. Gently sauté 3-4 minutes.

2. Sprinkle with flour, stir well and add wine, salt and pepper. Cook over low heat 2 minutes, then add cream. Bring mixture to a boil, reduce heat and simmer 5 minutes longer.

3. Spoon over pasta and serve with grated Parmesan cheese.

Makes 4 servings.

Each serving contains:

Cal	Prot	Carb	Fib	Tot. Fat	Sat. Fat	Chol	Sodium
365	20g	20g	1g	22g	13g	419mg	285mg

Vin Santo ~ *Vin Santo is a very rich, highly aromatic wine which is produced mainly in the Trentino and Tuscany. Made from grapes which have been dried in the sun, it is usually fairly sweet.*

MUSHROOM-AND-VEAL SAUCE

If you do not want to use veal, pork can be substituted. The sauce works well with most shapes but I particularly like to serve it with rotelle or wheels.

1 oz. (25g) dried mixed wild mushrooms

1 onion, peeled and minced

1 clove garlic, peeled and crushed

3 tablespoons olive oil

3/4 lb. (340g) ground veal or pork

2 tablespoons chopped fresh parsley

1 tablespoon chopped fresh sage or 1 teaspoon dried sage

1 teaspoon grated lemon peel

1/4 cup (60ml) red wine

1-2 tablespoons capers

1 teaspoon cornstarch

Cooked pasta to serve 4 people

Freshly grated Parmesan cheese

1. Cover mushrooms with boiling water and let stand for 15 minutes. Drain, reserving the liquid, and chop mushrooms.

2. Meanwhile sauté onion and garlic in oil until lightly browned. Add meat and cook, stirring, about 5 minutes.

3. Add parsley, sage, lemon peel, wine and capers and bring to a boil. Add chopped mushrooms and simmer 15 minutes.

4. Mix mushroom liquor with cornstarch and stir into sauce. Return to a boil and cook another 5-6 minutes.

5. Pour sauce over pasta and serve with freshly grated Parmesan cheese.

Makes 4 servings.

Each serving contains:

Cal	Prot	Carb	Fib	Tot. Fat	Sat. Fat	Chol	Sodium
435	29g	34g	3g	19g	5g	93mg	341mg

SESAME-CHICKEN SAUCE

Italians rarely use chicken in their pasta sauces while in the Far East chicken appears in many noodle dishes. In this East-meets-West sauce I have taken the best elements of both to make what has become one of my favorite supper dishes. I usually use farfalle and serve a salad of sliced raw sugar peas dressed with a simple vinaigrette.

3 tablespoons toasted sesame seeds

2 tablespoons cornstarch

Salt and pepper to taste

3 small skinless chicken breast fillets or 4 boned and skinned chicken thighs, cut into strips

3 tablespoons peanut or corn oil

1 teaspoon roasted sesame oil

6-8 green onions, trimmed and cut into 2-inch lengths

Grated peel and juice of 2 tangerines

1 tablespoon soy sauce

1/4 cup (60ml) Amontillado sherry

1/4 cup (60ml) chicken stock

Cooked pasta to serve 4 people

Fresh parsley sprigs

Variation

Use oranges instead of tangerines.

1. Mix toasted seeds with cornstarch, salt and pepper. Toss chicken strips in mixture to coat. Set remaining mix aside.

2. Heat oils in a wok or large deep skillet and sauté green onion and tangerine peel 1 minute. Add chicken strips and stir-fry over medium heat 2-3 minutes until cooked through.

3. Add remaining sauce ingredients, including tangerine juice and any leftover coating mix. Stir and bring to a boil. Cook two minutes longer.

4. Arrange pasta on four plates. Top with chicken mixture and garnish with parsley sprigs. Serve at once.

Makes 4 servings.

Each serving contains:

Cal	Prot	Carb	Fib	Tot. Fat	Sat. Fat	Chol	Sodium
421	27g	33g	2g	18g	3g	55mg	374mg

PANCETTA-AND-BEAN SAUCE

As with many of the best pasta sauces there are only a few ingredients in this sauce from Liguria. The secret of its success lies in the unique combination of flavors. I did a lot of experimenting to get it right. Serve with fusilli.

1/3 lb. (175g) smoked pancetta

2 tablespoons extra-virgin olive oil

1/2 teaspoon fennel seeds

4 small zucchini, trimmed and diced

1/3 cup (80ml) whipping cream

Salt and pepper to taste

1 can (14-oz. / 400g) white kidney beans, drained and rinsed

Cooked pasta to serve 4 people

1. Remove excess fat from pancetta and place pieces of fat in a large saucepan. Heat gently to release the fat. Remove pieces from pan.

2. Dice remaining pancetta. Add oil to fat in the saucepan and fry pancetta until lightly browned. Add fennel seeds and cook another minute or so. Add zucchini and toss with pancetta and fennel seeds over medium heat 3-4 minutes.

3. Add cream, salt and pepper. Bring to a boil. Add beans and cook another 1-2 minutes until heated through. Take care not to break beans when stirring.

4. Toss pasta with sauce and serve at once.

Makes 4 servings.

Each serving contains:

Cal	Prot	Carb	Fib	Tot. Fat	Sat. Fat	Chol	Sodium
413	19g	44g	6g	18g	7g	49mg	676mg

CALIFORNIA PORK SAUCE

This recipe was inspired by the unusual flavor combinations used by the chef of a nearby restaurant. He is quite happy to mix Scandinavian flavors with those of Thailand, or Caribbean ingredients with those of central Europe. So this is my attempt at a completely cosmopolitan sauce! Serve it with fusilli, rotelle or conchiglie.

3 tablespoons peanut or corn oil

3/4 lb. (340g) lean pork steaks, trimmed and cut into small dice

1 can (14-oz. / 400g) tomatoes

5-6 green onions, minced

1 red bell pepper, seeded and minced

1 piece (1-in. / 2.5cm) fresh ginger, peeled and grated

2 cloves garlic, peeled and crushed

Grated peel and juice of 1 lime

Salt and pepper to taste

1/2 cup (25g) fresh cilantro or coriander, chopped

Cooked pasta to serve 4 people

8-12 sprigs fresh cilantro or coriander

2 tablespoons toasted peanuts

1. Heat oil in a large pan and fry pork until lightly browned.

2. Add tomatoes and juice with remaining ingredients except cilantro or coriander, pasta and peanuts. Bring mixture to a boil, reduce heat and simmer 15 minutes, stirring occasionally.

3. Add chopped cilantro or coriander and cook 5 minutes longer.

4. Toss pasta with sauce, making sure that it is well coated. Serve garnished with sprigs of cilantro or coriander and toasted peanuts.

Makes 4 servings.

Each serving contains:

Cal	Prot	Carb	Fib	Tot. Fat	Sat. Fat	Chol	Sodium
459	31g	35g	3g	22g	5g	72mg	296mg

INDEX

Peas with Tomato and Basil 87
Provençale Sauce 33
Puttanesca Sauce 41
Rich Ricotta Sauce 105
Ricotta-and-Tomato Sauce 17
Sauce Norma 81
Sole in Tomato Sauce 69
Summer Sauce 88
Tuna-and-Tomato Sauce 38
Tuscan-Tomato-and-Basil Sauce
   27, 56
Vongole Sauce 40
tomatoes, sun-dried *see* sun-dried
   tomatoes
tonnarelli xv, 24
tortelloni 1
trenette xv, 20, 52, 54
trofie 74
tubular pasta xvi, 1, 7, 14, 16, 73-93
tuna 80, 111
   Tuna Sauce 37
   Tuna-and-Tomato Sauce 38
   Tuna with Shrimp 39
   Tuna-and-White-Bean Sauce 67
Turkish Tahini Sauce 101
Tuscan Lima-Bean Sauce 55
Tuscan Chickpea Sauce 70
Tuscan Pesto 58
Tuscan Tomato-and-Basil Sauce 27, 56

V
veal, ground
   Mushroom-and-Veal Sauce 117
Venetian Fish-and-Fennel Sauce 43
vermicelli xv, 16, 24, 32, 33
Vesuvio Sauce 19
vinegar, balsamic, *see* balsamic vinegar
Vin Santo 116
Vongole Sauce 38, 40

W
walnuts 17
   Goat-Cheese-and-Walnut Sauce 15
   Turkish Tahini Sauce 101
   Tuscan Pesto Sauce 58
   Salmon-and-Walnut Sauce 111
whiskey
   Mushrooms with Whiskey 61
white kidney beans, canned
   Pancetta-and-Bean Sauce 119

Tuna-and-White-Bean Sauce 67
wild mushrooms, *see* mushrooms, wild
wine, red 47, 92, 108, 117
   Chicken Livers with Leeks and
      Red Wine 48
wine, white 42, 70, 78, 89, 91, 108, 116
   Blue-Cheese-and-Broccoli Sauce 98
   Grass and Hay 72
   Monkfish-and-Tomato Sauce 112
   Salmon-and-Walnut sauce 111
   Salmon with Wine and Dill 68

Z
ziti xvi, 74, 76, 92
zucchini 67, 80, 119
   Spring Sauce 77
   Zucchini-and-Garlic Sauce 102
   Zucchini-and-Red-Onion Sauce 76

Quick After-Work Recipe Contest
Fisher Books
4239 W. Ina Road, #101
Tucson, AZ 85741

Enter the Quick After-Work Recipe Contest

Win more than $1,000 in cash and prizes!

The Quick After-Work Recipe Contest runs through August 31, 1996. Prizes will be announced by September 30, 1996. Entries are to be postmarked by August 31, 1996. All entries must be original recipes created by the contestant for the Quick After-Work Recipe Contest. Recipes cannot include ingredients that are brand-specific.

Entries can be one-dish suppers or dinners, main dishes, side dishes, appetizers or desserts. We encourage supplemental menus and anecdotes about special quick after-work meals and experiences.

Grand prize: $500 cash, a library of Fisher Books cookbooks, plus a pasta machine and a food processor. The winning recipe will be published in a future *Quick After-Work* cookbook.

Second prize: $200 cash, a library of Fisher Books cookbooks, a pasta machine and a food processor.

Purchase is not required for entry. One entry per person. Entries will be judged by Helen Fisher and a panel of cookbook authors and Fisher Books editors. Winners will be required to sign a publicity release and a certificate of eligibility and to give permission to reprint the recipe in various media. All recipes become the property of Fisher Books and will not be returned. The contestant's name, address and phone number must be submitted with the recipe.

Mail your entry to: Quick After-Work Recipe Contest
4239 W. Ina Road, #101
Tucson, AZ 85741

Name _____

Address _____

City/State/ZIP _____

Phone _____

Store where book was purchased _____

Entries must be postmarked by August 31, 1996.